ACHIEVING A BETTER
WORLD FOR EVERY PERSON

Inspired by the joint legacy of
Nathan and Esther K. Wagner

Copyright © 2020
bioGraph LLC

bioGraphbook.com

BIOGRAPH LLC

Published by bioGraph
Chicago, IL
bioGraphbook.com

First bioGraph trade paperback edition December 2019

For information about discounts for bulk purchases,
please contact info@bioGraphbook.com

Designed by bioGraph
Manufactured in the United States of America
3 4 5 6 7 8 9 10

Printed on 90gsm acid-free paper

ISBN: 978-1-951946-04-3 (paperback)
ISBN: 978-1-951946-05-0 (eBook)

IT'S NOT ABOUT ME

I am not your teacher, and I'm not smarter than you, but I've had some experiences, which I can hopefully translate in helpful ways. While I am providing "pathways and processes" to help each of you reach your goals, all actions required must be your own.

To optimize the gift of life we have received, I recommend these two everlasting truths:

★ Practice enlightened self-interest by recognizing that your own interests are best served in win-win situations where all parties benefit.

★ Love is the ultimate form of enlightened self-interest and the most important and fulfilling dynamic on earth. As my wife always said, "Love life, love people, be sincere and never cease striving to make the world better for every person."

Table of Contents

Prologue

The narrative presented herein is replete with themes, observations and conclusions that reflect my personal life experience and what has worked successfully for me to achieve a life that was more fulfilling than what I could ever have hoped for. However, my story would not be the whole truth if I did not acknowledge how much I have learned and gained from observing the moving forces that were the essence of my wife Esther's life that were, and still are, so constructive in living a fulfilled life for everyone. Accordingly, I present the following as <u>our joint life legacy</u>:

<u>*"Love life, love people, be sincere and never cease striving to make the world better for every person"*</u>

This world, and the life that exists within it, is one of the most amazing realities of which one can conceive. The questions that it raises to many people are "<u>how did it come to be</u>?" and, since life for each individual is for a limited amount of time, "<u>what</u>

1

should one do to make life as fulfilling as possible while it lasts?" The first question may never be answerable, however, the second question is a matter that we *CAN and SHOULD do something about.*

We are writing this narrative in an attempt to demonstrate what any and every person can do to enhance the wonderful gift of life that they were given. My wife and I were fortunate in being part of life for a combined total of over 175 years. During that period, we were able to observe the lives of so many other people who found effective pathways to optimize their time on earth.

We do not claim any unique knowledge on the subject, however, we do believe that the numerous opportunities we were able to see, in how life worked for the better of so many others, is valuable research from which some of us can find a pathway that works best for us. This is one area where the following adage really applies:

"WE GET OLDER TOO SOON AND WISER TOO LATE"

However, just like in science, we should stand upon the shoulders of others who preceded us and build upon the knowledge they found that enhanced their lives and could do the same for those who follow.

So...let us proceed:

Man was once defined as follows:

"The only 150-pound complex servo-mechanism that is mass-produced by unskilled labor"

While the foregoing is phrased in a somewhat humorous form, it has a lot of truth in it. In addition, each new-born comes into life also unskilled and without any ability to think or even to sustain its own existence unless help is forthcoming from others. In effect, each of us comes into a world that is hostile to our survival unless other human beings pitch in to meet our needs at birth and in so many other ways as we grow.

This brings us to the next question:

"What are the goals and propensities of this world that we all inherit and will be part of?"

It is well-established that human beings are, first and foremost, motivated by a sense of *perceived per-*

sonal self-interest that will dominate their thinking, decisions and actions for as long as they live. Accordingly, new generations become part of a very competitive world that has limited resources and that makes the following question relevant:

> *"What methods should be adopted to share earth's available resources in the most efficacious way?"*

The foregoing question presents a constant challenge to those people who want to take actions in life to advance their personal interests and goals. Since the existing world is based upon the dynamics of perceived personal self-interest, such people must be able to demonstrate that their desired actions will also concurrently benefit the personal interests of any other people who may be affected. Our life experience, personally and professionally, has convinced us that the most successful pathway to enhance our own self-interest was when we consistently provided value-added services that advance the self-interest of others. In other words, *the self-interest that we seek for ourselves can best be attained when we help others to concurrently enhance their own self-interest*. We call this concept *ENLIGHTENED SELF-INTEREST*.

One purpose of this narrative is to outline concepts where persons and societies could, in a most constructive way, _work individually and collectively toward a goal where all parties become winners_ and not a world where, for one party to win, the other party must lose _(a zero-sum result)._

A self-enlightened world, where "ALL" are winners, is immeasurably better.

To achieve the foregoing, we will comment firstly on basic concepts from which we have evolved actions and themes that are presented later in a listing of _"Factors that Matter in Achieving a Better World for Every Person."_ The following are three _thematic summaries_ of the foregoing "Factors" that we will address below. The individual "Factors" will be expounded upon later in various sections of this book.

(1) **GOAL - - - Our existing and new generations must be better educated to become a reasoned, well-informed and action-oriented electorate.**

We strongly believe that the prime responsibility of parents is to prepare their children adequately for the **"REAL"** adult world that they will be entering. In that REAL world, the main moving forces that affect people's lives are political, economic and value systems; the actual behavior of humankind, and knowledge of which past societal actions have been shown to be constructive or ineffective.

Unfortunately, a very high percentage of our existing population is currently poorly educated and remains ill-informed with respect to how these major moving forces will have the greatest impact on the quality of their lives. In addition, the existing education systems are clearly inadequate (in content and exposure time) to alter this existing reality. Our urgent need is to educate the majority of our citizens to make reasoned decisions about different political and economic systems, to know as much as possible about what history teaches us and to understand the nature of humankind and what it is prone to do. *These issues matter!!!*

Sadly, while we should be prioritizing the

above matters that have so much impact on life, the current focus of most of our people is on high-tech gadgets that primarily promote social interaction. These people are mainly responsive to "spin" and "headlines" (not facts) to form their judgments on how to achieve a better life for all people.

(2) <u>GOAL - - - Optimize life in our competitive world by actively promoting constructive individual and collective societal action to attain desired goals.</u>

The importance of one person, in a world filled with billions of people, would appear to be minimal. However, contemporary life, with its existing social communication systems, has shown many examples where a new light or idea, originated by only a few people, can grow to be endorsed by millions in a relatively short period of time. Therefore, we believe that everyone should maintain a *<u>positive-outlook lifestyle</u>* that emphasizes how each person can contribute to achieving a better world

7

in this life for everyone.

As we concluded earlier, the self-interest we seek for ourselves can best be attained when we help others to concurrently enhance their own self-interest. _So...how do we proceed?_ With the foregoing as a goal, everyone should sincerely plan their life-activities so as to be seen as a person who _"adds value"_ to whatever projects with which they are involved. They should also invite others to share their opportunities and they should use every occasion possible to elevate the self-image of others.

Our life experience convinces us that if a person sincerely follows an _"added-value" lifestyle_, they will become highly admired by others who, in turn, will seek out that person to share in opportunities that would not otherwise have been available. Accordingly, the efforts by everyone to achieve a more-fulfilled life would be greatly enhanced.

(3) <u>GOAL - - - Strive to build positive relation-ships with others and live a life of which you are proud.</u>

Life has a vast number of elements and dynamics that interface with each person throughout their life. Some of these are favorable and some are not. Nevertheless, the most important thing to always bear in mind is that each of these happenings are not of the same importance. A lump in the cereal or a lump in one's throat or a lump in one's breast are not of the same magnitude. Maintaining perspective and establishing priorities, by quantifying the relative importance of all happenings, is critical to optimizing one's existence (physically and psychologically) as well as building a more constructive co-existence with the other people with whom one is sharing life.

Without diminishing any of the foregoing, the dynamics of love, family relationships and health are the most fulfilling and should be emphasized the most throughout one's life on earth.

POSITIVE MENTAL ATTITUDE (PMA)

While we have heretofore been detailing the importance of taking actions that we strongly believe will benefit individuals and society, there is one overriding perspective that is foundational for each of us to more fully realize our life goals and objectives. Life happenings are things over which we have very little control. The only thing we can control is how we react to what life presents to us from time-to-time. A wise man once wrote as follows:

> **"The remarkable thing is that we have a choice every day regarding the attitude we will embrace for that day. We cannot change our past...we cannot change the fact that people will act in a certain way. We cannot change the inevitable. The only thing we can do is play on the one string we have, and that is our attitude...I am convinced that life is 10% what happens to me and 90% how I react to it. And, so it is with you...we are in charge of our attitudes."**

An important thought we can add is that **PMA** can often, <u>*with creative thinking,*</u> make what originally appears to be a negative happening turn into a positive result. Maintaining **PMA** can make all the difference in the quality of life that one would be able to enjoy and then pass on. At birth, we learn only to "see," not necessarily to "understand." Ours is an endless challenge to search out wisdom and the "unseen" from the hidden depths so that they may brighten and enlighten our lives.

Lastly, it may sound Pollyannaish, but we firmly believe that having a positive attitude is essential to living and enjoying a successful life. Positivity perpetuates itself and truly makes a difference. <u>**So**</u>...our advice to you is to **make a habit of taking a glass half-full approach to life.**

<u>Now</u> - - - Some of my personal thoughts on how to achieve the better world that we are seeking.

Personal Thoughts

I believe that this narrative is very different than anything that you have ever encountered, since it focuses primarily on core principles that have added value to _MY LIFE_ in the world that we all share. I hope, in turn, that it will add value to yours. This is not about me; this is not a tutorial on how to live well and thrive in business that is authored by someone supposed to know best. I am not your teacher and I am not smarter than you. However, I have had some long-life experiences that have manifested in ways that I can now articulate and that could help each of you as you travel through _YOUR LIFE_.

Why should you care? If not for pure curiosity or love of knowledge, then because it may be in your personal _"enlightened self-interest."_ What does my life have to do with yours and the lives of others? Well, just about everything. No man is an island. Each person is a part of humankind, and what that person endures will likely be experienced by multitudes of others as well.

If you look at the world as it exists, you'll find that *"enlightened self-interest"* (ESI) is not very widely acknowledged or practiced. When you want any other person to join into any activity that you are proposing, that other person's reaction is normally to think: *"where is my piece and how will I benefit?"* The challenge is then finding the most efficacious way of achieving your goals while also contributing to a better world for others. That is what truly works and is the basic dynamic that I am trying to address.

Most of what I will say concerns what I have learned from history. Unfortunately, the records of humankind show that *what we learn from history is that "we don't learn from history."* This is a disastrous reality. **We must learn from history about causes and their effects, about actions and reactions and about consequences that are intended and unintended.** If people had to learn anew in every generation, we would never progress. Language, culture and civilization exist because past generations provided wisdom. So, let's now talk about life in the current world.

My experience has convinced me that life need not be a zero-sum game and that **win-win outcomes**

are achievable through the use of _Enlightened Self-interest._ I call myself **a REALIST**, because I base my reasoning and actions on what I found actually worked in the **REAL** world. Additionally, since I am a realist, I must possess a degree of skepticism that I learned from living in the **REAL** world. When I first look at any matter, I try to get an overall picture of a situation, but I never conclude and say **"This is it."** I must get more deeply into the details to assure myself that what I see is accurate and comprehensive. In addition to being a realist, I have embraced two tenets with which I have lived my life. Firstly, to strive, with a positive outlook, toward shaping events that are happening (both in and out of my control) and secondly, to strive to creatively achieve win-win outcomes wherever possible.

As a country, we've had a pretty good run, arguably one of the best in human history. I am grateful to have had a front row seat for much of U.S. history and to have played my part in making our democracy work. As I look back on my long and fruitful life, I'd like to share a few reflections in the hope that it will do some good for you and others.

I am a product of an era where Morse code was

the most efficient mode of communication, when you could ride the streetcar in Chicago for seven cents and when commercial airlines were just getting off the ground. It makes my head spin to think about the dramatic changes I have lived through. So many advances in technology, communications, transportation and medicine have immensely altered life for the better and will continue to do so for many years to come.

Yet, I am very concerned about the state of affairs in America and its future. I worry that we are losing our competitive edge and I am troubled about a growing social apathy and an inadequate educational system. I fear that we are currently in the process of pawning our future for short-term gains and when the bill comes due, we won't have the means to pay it.

So...what can be done about all, or any, of the concerns which I have referenced? Do Americans have the wherewithal to confront these challenges and come up with solutions? Or, have a sizeable number of Americans become complacent (and dependent upon government) and are assuming that their present way of life will always be the same? I can't give you the answers, but I can offer you the following truisms *(with certainty of their validity)* that *must* be pursued for the future in order to maintain the viability of our culture and current way of life:

a. **A more realistic education of new and existing generations about the "*REAL WORLD*" so that society's members can play a more meaningful role in politics IS KEY.**

b. **Reasoned affirmative-action by a well-informed electorate IS ESSENTIAL.**

c. **The utilization of enlightened self-interest (ESI) by a larger percentage of our population and maintaining a positive outlook to achieve a better life for all people IS CRITICAL.**

I firmly believe that the efforts to safeguard a better world for the future must come from the bottom up *(the individual citizen)* and not from the top down *(the elected leaders)*.

A realistic and truly meaningful education enriches life, provides perspective, encourages creativity, increases opportunity, opens minds and opens doors. *Well-educated and well-informed citizens are an essential foundation* in order to build a productive society that is able to thrive and compete in a constantly changing world.

Winston Churchill once said, "Democracy is the worst form of government, except for all the others." He was right! As imperfect as democracy is, it offers the best chance for liberty, equality, opportunity and upward mobility through hard work. But democracy can only be maintained by active participation of society where "_We the People_" are always involved and continually striving for a **more perfect union**.

History repeats itself and I implore all of you to avoid repeating the mistakes of the past. Don't ignore history; study it for enlightenment and life lessons. If you truly want to optimize life for yourself and others, then focus on building upon the knowledge and work of those who came before you in a way that will also benefit those who come after you.

History convinces me that success in planning is most likely to be achieved if the following process is taken *(in the order listed)* <u>*to achieve goals and reach consensus within any group that has multiple decision-makers.*</u>

a. First, identify the goals, relevant problems and challenges that must be overcome. <u>*(Obtain consensus before proceeding to step "B")*</u>

b. Secondly, list the various factors that could alleviate or solve the foregoing problems and challenges and evaluate each factor for its potential efficacy. <u>*(Obtain consensus before proceeding to step "C")*</u>

c. Finally, establish the criteria by which suggested solutions will be judged and adopted. <u>*(Obtain consensus on all of the foregoing matters before proceeding to final decision-making)*</u>

If I were asked to implement the foregoing methodology for achieving a better world, I would likely prepare the following outline:

a. *Our goal should be to make the world happier and more fulfilling for every person.* Our problems and challenges are that the natural instincts of people (personal self-interest) make our goal extremely difficult to achieve, and the world does not have the resources to give each and every person everything they may desire from time to time.

b. Then I would propose to convince as many people as possible to adopt and personally implement the list of *"Factors that Matter in Achieving A Better World for Every Person"* that appears later herein.

c. Since perfection is unattainable, I believe that *the best we can hope for are world systems and societies that work in a way that provides the greatest good for the greatest number of people.* Remember! ... You can never fully satisfy every person and you will surely fail if you try.

Perfection is the Enemy of the Good

We will now proceed to *"Factors that Matter in Achieving A Better World for Every Person."* I strongly believe that if enough people adopt these "Factors" into their way of life, we will attain the goals we are seeking. Each of the "Factors" I list relate to issues upon which libraries have shelves overflowing with books already written with many more books to come. Accordingly, it would be arrogant and presumptuous if I felt able to add great value to any of the "Factors." **So,** what I will do is set forth all of the "Factors" that I am convinced are essential moving forces in achieving our goals and then add comments on why I selected them and why I may have chosen some elements from each of them that I felt would also contribute to advancing our goals.

The following list of fundamentals, themes and actions make up the "Factors" that are essential concomitants for us to realize what we can do while we are still part of

THIS DREAM WE CALL LIFE

Factors that Matter

In Achieving a Better World For Every Person

Pathways to enhance the well-being of all people

1. **Educating the public to develop a reasoning society and electorate:**
   a. Political systems *(Understanding historical advantages and shortcomings)*
   b. Economic systems *(Understanding historical advantages and shortcomings)*
   c. Enlightened self-interest *(One's self-interest is best served when all parties are winners)*
   d. Parenting *(Raising children with proper outlook on entitlement and personal responsibility)*
   e. Promote a highly moral society *(Guided by existing equitable monotheism principles)*
   f. Society must arrange to *meet the needs of the unfortunate but not necessarily their wants*

g. Philosophy, Psychology and the Real World (_Understanding human nature, propensities of humankind and creating ways to achieve a more perfect world for every person_)

2. **Living in a competitive world with limited resources:**
   a. _Add all the value that one is able to_ whatever activity with which one is involved
   b. Identify the _personal agendas of co-workers, and seek to enhance these wherever possible_
   c. Have all of one's activities recognize _the importance of personal responsibility and ethics_
   d. Educate yourself to invest wisely to enhance _financial assets for the present and the future_
   e. Make sure that reasoning has been completed before the mouth is put into action
   f. Recognize that _our only choice in life_

is to _make the best of what is actually available to us_

g. When reason and emotion conflict, _allow reason to prevail wherever possible_

h. To achieve goals and preserve values, _affirmative action must overcome complacency_

i. Reasoned perseverance, honesty and sincerity have _the best winning record to achieve goals_

j. In debates, _articulateness is critical; words (that are not quantifiable) do not serve well_

3. **Relationships with others, family and general conduct:**

a. Every person is unique and is deserving of respect and personal parity in all regards

b. One should focus on _reinforcing the self-image of others_ with whom one is associated

c. Reason carefully — _immediate-gratification vs. deferred-gratification (Life is_ *a balance sheet)*

d. *Family and love are the most fulfilling elements of life* and should be emphasized accordingly

e. A person inheriting and adopting a *legacy is a link in a chain* and should strive to *pass such legacy on undiminished*

f. *Only* the role-model by which one lives and the legacy one leaves endure in time

Political Systems

Historical advantages and shortcomings

Politics to me is the essence of life. It pervades everything. Politics is ubiquitous: a dynamic, living, motive force that can be harnessed to enhance the quality of our lives. Politics polices the bounds of our liberty, but in return it protects our nourishment and promotes our flourishing. Humans are born into a world of fire, flood, disease, and hunger. We must compete as well as cooperate among ourselves and other creatures for a share of the planet's scarce resources. The establishment of political systems first arose from the need to cope with the hostile environment we call earth.

Emerging from the State of Nature

The seventeenth-century philosopher Thomas Hobbes imagined the state of nature (that is, the natural state of human existence before the establishment of government) as having "no arts; no letters; no society; and, which is worst of all, continual fear and danger of violent death; and the life of man solitary, poor, nasty, brutish, and short." This state of nature is no utopian garden of Eden, but rather a dehumanizing "war of all against all" where "man is wolf to man." On the bright side, Hobbes also declared that *"the first and fundamental law of nature" is to "seek peace and follow it."* It's therefore natural for living beings to organize themselves into structures that promote survival, stability, and peace. Human government is one such structure.

It didn't take long for the earliest humans to realize the benefits of cooperation when it came to surviving, coping with and overcoming a world of forces both conducive and inimical to life itself. In addition to hunger and extreme climatic events, humans had to avoid becoming prey to stronger species that hunted them as well as provide protection from other humans who would not hesitate to ravage their fellow humans to advance their own *perceived* self-interest.

In Isaiah Berlin's words, the time had come "when men and women would take their lives in their own hands and not be self-seeking beings or the playthings of blind forces that they did not understand." Humans emerged from the state of nature by organizing into governmental structures. One of the earliest classifications of government was the tribal system, whereby a few (the **ELITE**) acquired power to rule over a much larger group comprised of the remaining members of the tribe (the **MASSES**). While there have been variations in the forms of government over the last several thousand years, the tribal system has prevailed as the most common form of organization in modern times. Consequently, the world's population is now mostly ruled by the **ELITES** *(selected by various means and criteria)* who rule over the **MASSES** using the following forms of government.

Democratically-Prone vs. Authoritarian-Prone Political Systems

As a realist who never claims to have the full picture of reality, I've never said, "So-and-so's a democrat, So-and-so's a republican, So-and-so's this, or So-and-so's that—because such character-izations essentialize and ossify forces that are, in reality, dynamic and subject to change. Once we define something in absolute terms, once we forget that the only thing permanent is change, then we become complacent.

I believe there exist two diametric categories of government: **DEMOCRATIC** and **AUTHORITAR-IAN**. While no one country falls completely under one or the other political system, if we account for the rights each system affords to its members, it helps us evaluate their fundamental differences. Democratically-prone governments have freedom of speech and majority rule, while maintaining the rights of minorities, equality of opportunity, fair elections, and comprehensive equality before the rule of law. Conversely, authoritarian-prone governments have few or even only one ruler, restricted freedoms, total obedience, and neither political representation nor social mobility for the voiceless masses, and citizens lack free and fair elections and have little political voice. Key attributes for these two forms of government are summarized in the following table.

Democratically-Prone Political Systems Include the Following Principal Elements	Authoritarian-Prone Political Systems Include the Following Principal Elements
Freedoms of speech, protest, religion and the press with minimal government interference	Freedoms of speech, protest, religion and the press are controlled by the government
Majority rule with recognized minority rights to protect against "tyranny by the majority"	Government rules and controls everything and protection of minority rights is not addressed
Citizens have free and fair competitive elections	Citizens lack free and fair elections
Citizen participation is required in order to maintain balance between rights and responsibilities	Citizens must obey, but have no voice in, government decision-making
There are few restrictions preventing any person from achieving political leadership	Leaders come from one small group (i.e. the military, the oligarchy or aristocratic families)
Rule of law is applicable to leaders and citizens equally	One ruler (or a small group of leaders) has the real power

Rather than say we live in a democracy, I find it more accurate to say we live in a democratically-prone political system. We must not be lulled by a failing education system, and by our own complacency, into believing that we live in a democracy once and for all, happily ever after, until the end of time. No nation falls entirely into either category and both types of government change over time. Some democracies have some authoritarian elements and vice-versa. A democratically-prone society can become an authoritarian-prone society over time, if not overnight.

Authoritarian-prone political systems tend to be socialistic, communistic or dictatorial. Despite what we've gone through in the last century, we haven't learned all the lessons we need to learn. Of course, the younger generation did not experience or witness the failure of socialist societies, but we must be students of history. Under every situation that you can think of, when people have put their faith in a socialist system (which _always requires_ an authoritarian government) that promised something for nothing, the next thing you know, millions of people have died. I can give you examples. The greatest socialist movements in the last 100 years have been Nazi, Russian, Venezuelan, and Chinese socialism. Outside of China, they (and many such smaller societies) have all been disastrous and complete failures. At this point, China's success or failure with its form of socialism (which it has combined with an authoritarian-prone political system and a free-market-prone economic system) remains to be seen. No matter how many times socialism claims to provide utopian results to everybody, it has inevitably and miserably failed. **History has proven that there are no free lunches in politics or in life.**

Liberty and Equality for All (Which cannot exist concurrently)

The relative degrees of individual liberty and equality among members are the most important dynamics affecting the ultimate viability of all societies. Liberty comes naturally, but equality does not. Isaiah Berlin put it poignantly:

> *Both liberty and equality are among the primary goals pursued by human beings throughout many centuries; but total liberty for wolves is death to the*

lambs, total liberty of the powerful, the gifted, is not compatible with the rights to a decent existence of the weak and the less gifted.

Equality in life requires some outside force to compensate for the fact that people are not born with equal physical or mental capabilities, they may not be born in environments or societies that offer comparable opportunities, and they are not born with equal assets. Accordingly, equality cannot be naturally achieved without some outside force that compels it. If someone has less of something that the society believes should be equal, then force must be used to take that something from another person whose liberty is thereby diminished. **Therefore, when more equality is desired, more liberty must be lost and when more liberty is desired, then more equality must be lost.**

Government produces nothing. It is just a re-distributor of wealth (after taking its share). It only takes from one person and gives it to another person. You must always bear this in mind, no matter what system you have. After thousands of years of evaluating what impact government has on the well-being of a society, most respected historians and philosophers have summarized its performance with some of the following highlights:

Positive results of government's collective strength in numbers:

a. It provides better protection against the dangers of life in a hostile world than any individual can do alone (i.e. extreme climate, disease, other nations, etc.)

b. It creates developments that are beyond the capacity of smaller groups of people (i.e. roads, airports, etc.)

c. It facilitates the viability and endurance of a competitive society to function effectively (i.e. by providing law and order, implementing justice, establishing morals, providing for the weak and disabled, etc.)

No one questions that government is essential for a society; however, it also comes with the following undesirables:

Negative features that come along with government:

a. It operates very inefficiently and is

excessively expensive.

b. It is replete with very costly political and economic corruption that undermines its ability to perform the good things that it is otherwise capable of doing.

c. Politicians continuously promise free benefits from government funds (*to obtain votes from the citizens*) which cumulatively and ultimately cause the fiscal collapse of the government with resultant anarchy and super-inflation, commonly followed by a dictatorship.

d. The **MASSES** become so addicted and dependent on the government that, whenever a significant problem presents, the battle cry goes out "*we gotta have a law to solve this problem.*" As a result, _ALL_ governments grow bigger and bigger in time and ultimately fail when their costs exceed their potential revenue sources.

Ergo, these same respected historians and philosophers conclude:

"That Government is Best that Governs Least"

Government is a necessary evil and people tend to call upon it much too much. I see that our country is becoming ever more complacent, apathetic, and dependent. Concurrently, I see our social and press media engaging in more and more advocacy and becoming "_news-MAKERS_" instead of being "_news-REPORTERS_." Our population is now increasingly receptive to spin and headlines (_instead of facts_) and it has become easy for social and press media to sway the uneducated and misinformed **MASSES** like feathers for every wind that blows.

It is **OUR** duty to **EDUCATE** our society about this permanent struggle between liberty and equality. Government requires voluntary forfeiture of, as well as involuntary encroachment upon, individual liberties and freedoms for the sake of collective peace, security, and some "_fair_" form of equality. Without this understanding, society will never be harmonious. Government's task and challenge is to strike a delicate balance, through laws and institutions, to maintain social harmony without neglecting any individual or group. *Compounding the challenge, everyone has a different definition of equality. Some mean equality under the law, others mean equality of financial income and/or outcome, some mean equality of opportunity and others believe that we should find some new form of being "fair."*

But what is "*fair*"? How should we quantify that word? What's the difference between what is "*right*" and what we should believe is "*fair*"? The *ill-educated masses* have not been adequately enlightened to think critically about words, which are not quantifiable. In democratically-prone societies, people have the right and responsibility to debate definitions in order to establish laws promoting the majority's conception of equality. In authoritarian-prone societies, equality is solely defined and implemented by the leader.

Unfortunately, there is no perfect system, but we must continue striving toward perfection. The pursuit of perfection requires seeing the unseen and studying history to learn what has worked in the past. The last 243 years of world history suggest that democracies which adopt "equality before the law" (like the USA) tend to strike the best balance for the future well-being of their members.

The United States of America was established in 1776 with no army or wealth. It was like a newborn baby among nations, yet, look what it has accomplished in fewer than three of my lifetimes.

    a. It defeated the then-existing most powerful world power in war to gain its independence.

    b. It endured a civil war during which about a half-million of its citizens were killed.

    c. It survived multiple severe economic downturns while maintaining peace in its society.

    d. It was a major military force in winning two world wars, preserving democracies and establishing a world order.

    e. It raised more people out of poverty than any other government in history.

    f. It increased its population by more than 50 times since its inception.

    g. It tripled its land size since its inception.

    h. It currently holds more than 1/3 of the

world's total wealth.

i. It built and maintains the most powerful military in the world.

j. It attracts people from all over the world
who are seeking to emigrate there for a
better life.

k. It transferred political power _peacefully_
44 times, even during wars and other
crises.

This impressive track record proves how
extraordinary and viable the American political
system is. Still, many among us believe our
system is imperfect and, in some respects, they are
correct. Establishing a more perfect union involves
a permanent struggle between liberty for all and
some form of equality amongst all. Our founders
understood this, and so they drafted a democratic
Constitution that gives the people power to find
over time what they hope will be the best balance
between liberty and equality. When societies have
erred in their efforts to appropriately balance liberty
and equality, they have done better when they have
erred on the side of greater liberty. History has

shown that when people put equality ahead of liberty, they usually end up losing both.

A Republic

Political systems are fragile enough for a single calamity to wipe out decades, and even centuries of progress. To remain viable, *a Democratic society MUST HAVE a WELL-EDUCATED and WELL-IN-FORMED ELECTORATE that is PROACTIVE and IM-BUED WITH ENLIGHTENED SELF-INTEREST*.

Just because liberty and equality can never be on the same plane does not mean that we are doomed to play a zero-sum game. It is in our self-interest to create and maintain political systems that promote win-win outcomes when opposing views in society are in conflict. It is also in our self-interest to preserve our political system for future generations, lest we become broken links in an otherwise unbroken chain. Remember the burning of the Library of Alexandria? All it takes is myopia and complacency to burn all our accrued wisdom into dust.

As I have stated earlier, one of the major mistakes that humankind is constantly repeating is its failure to learn from the lessons of history. The world may be millions of years old, however, new people are born with each new generation. *It is foolhardy and illogical for us to require each new generation of people to learn anew how to best manage its affairs when it can best learn from what has worked and what has not worked from the past.*

Our generation has been blessed by the thousands of generations that preceded us who faced challenges in this hostile world that we would have hated to have had to face ourselves. Yet, they survived and prevailed in coping with their challenges and in starting a process of learning more about this world that they were able to pass onto future generations. Visionary people are then able to stand on their ancestors' shoulders and build likewise for generations that will follow them. During that time, regimes all around the world have evolved and changed. The Soviet Union rose and fell, and the sun set on the British Empire. Any civilization can feasibly collapse within three generations or much less.

Alexander Fraser Tyler wrote "The Decline and Fall of the Athenian Republic" in 1770 after studying democracies that had existed in the past thousand years. He concluded that *Democracy is not a permanent form of government and that the average length of life of a democracy is 200 years.* He also found that *every democratic republic went through each of the following stages* in the sequence shown:

From bondage to spiritual faith;
From spiritual faith to great courage;
From courage to liberty;
From liberty to abundance;
From abundance to complacency;
From complacency to apathy;
From apathy to dependence;
From dependence back into bondage.

We must heed and react to the reality of Tyler's foregoing sequence of cyclical progression according to which **ALL** democratic republics have passed, so that we do not become another historical statistic.

Consider, again, that our country is already 43 years over the average life of a democracy and, in my opinion, our *current apathy* has us trapped somewhere between *complacency and dependence (as shown above).* To avoid the inevitable backslide into bondage, much effort and time is required, and we're already late in starting.

The time to act is NOW !!!

Immortalized in the United States Holocaust Memorial Museum is the Lutheran pastor Martin Niemöller's poetic warning that the horrors of the Holocaust were enabled by *political apathy and perceived self-interest*. "First, they came for the Socialists, and I did not speak out—Because I was not a Socialist." This formula continues as the Nazis come for trade unionists and Jews, until finally, "they came for me—and there was no one left to speak for me." In the face of never-ending domestic political upheaval, genocide, terrorism, and the resurgence of nationalism and fascism, however, it is tempting to focus on these transitional problems and not see the danger to our way of life that lies ahead. *We must not again fail to learn history's lessons and let our apathy cause us to not see, and deal with, the current existential danger before it's too late.*

With enlightened self-interest and righteous urgency Hillel the Elder asked, "If I am not for myself, who is for me? And being for my own self, what am 'I'? And if not now, when?" We must not trade our hoped-for long-term peace for instant gratification, just as we mustn't save for tomorrow what we can do today.

In the period during which the USA Constitution was being considered for adoption, someone asked Benjamin Franklin (one of our senior Founding Fathers) the following question:

What kind of government are you giving us?
His answer was . . . .

"A Republic, ... *IF YOU CAN KEEP IT"*

Our focus and prime interest must be to ensure
Franklin's legacy, and not squander the essential,
but fragile, political system that is giving us such
an exceptional present life and has even greater
possibilities for the future.

Economic Systems

Understanding historical
advantages and shortcomings

Since man appeared on this earth, his instincts and needs compelled him to join with other humans for survival and for accessing the benefits that are attainable in this world. This created a challenge of how to develop a reward system to compensate participants equitably for the disparate value that each person contributed to the joint efforts. The answer was to create a system called economics. From such a beginning, and continuing to the present, as the condition of humankind's world changed, the systems that were used also changed (scores of times) to what was perceived to be more effective for the *"REAL"* world that existed from time to time.

Like politics, religion, and other human-designed systems, economics profoundly shapes our lives in the short and long term. Accordingly, we have a responsibility to educate ourselves as much as possible on the relative advantages and shortcomings of different systems. All members of each society should make every effort to learn about how well any system is working and what its effect is on everyone's well-being. *We must learn what has worked in the past and what has failed, if we are to better understand what will likely work best now and in the future.*

Practically all world economic systems existing today fall into two classifications. Most of the world uses a system called "**CAPITALISM**" and a smaller group uses variations of what is called "**SOCIALISM.**" Although, each system incorporates some elements or variations of the other system, they are significantly different from each other and have substantially different impacts on how their members are benefitted or disadvantaged.

Notes on the origin of today's economic systems and their outcomes to date

In its purest forms, capitalism is an economic social system where government is exclusively devoted to the protection of individual and property rights and where government does not intervene in the economy. Over the centuries, there have been many variations of capitalism that dealt differently with individual rights and government's role. What has evolved from the foregoing are two broad schools of thought that dominate today's world and are diametrically opposed to each other.

One school is associated with economic liberalism (*as set forth by Adam Smith in the 18th century*), who believed that capitalism is an expression of natural human behavior because it emphasizes personal liberty, frees people to exercise their creative and innovative entrepreneurial nature, and is the most beneficial way of promoting human well-being. Economic liberalism is the essence of modern-day <u>Capitalism</u>.

A significantly smaller second school (*founded by Karl Marx*) views capitalism as a system of economic relationships between classes that should be replaced by other systems that would better serve human well-being by achieving more equality of economic results with more restrictions on individual liberty. That school sees capitalism as originating in more powerful people potentially taking control of the means of production and compelling others to sell their labor as a commodity. That is the essence of modern-day <u>*Socialism*</u>.

As I stated in the section on "political systems,"

no society has a pure Democratic political system or a pure Authoritarian political system. Each political system has adopted some elements of the other to accommodate each society's perceived special needs. This lack of "pure" political systems is also true with respect to economic systems.

We have ended up today with **Capitalistically-prone** economic systems and **Socialistically-prone** economic systems. Accordingly, I will outline on the following pages the more significant features of both systems now in use, along with a brief comment on how each feature was implemented by each system.

ANALYSIS OF ECONOMIC SYSTEMS

Feature	Capitalism	Socialism
Economic principles (those that should be compatible with human nature to be successful)	Emphasizes individual rights and equality of opportunity but not equality of results	Emphasizes various forms of economic equality of results accompanied by significant limitation of each individual's liberty
Means of Production	Mostly privately owned	Mainly government-owned or controlled
Pricing	Free open-market forces control	All pricing matters are determined by government
Competition	Exists to a very high degree	Exists only to a very low degree
Efficiency	Maximized (by being based mainly on incentives)	Minimized (by being based mainly on accountability)
Government Control	None or reasonably marginal	Government decides almost everything

Feature	Capitalism	Socialism
Wealth and Income	Each person works for the creation of his own wealth	Shared by all of society's members based upon various forms of perceived fairness

While all the features outlined above are significant, it is critical to understand that _most of these features_ ("_economic principles_") _are implemented by statutory laws_ that are legally enforceable upon the citizens. The **ELITE** of each system customizes each of the features shown with their unique and relevant incentives or disincentives that they hope will motivate the **MASSES** to act in a manner that the **ELITE** of each system believes would result in the economy achieving the **ELITE's** desired economic goals.

However, we must understand that "Economics" is not a science and we should bear in mind that, based upon history, any course of action that is recommended to people _must be compatible with human instincts and nature if it is to be successfully implemented by people and prevail over time._ In other words, history shows that "_economic principles_" have always prevailed over statutory laws that are not compatible with human nature and instincts.

Long live Economic Principles!!!

ACCORDINGLY, society should adopt only those economic principles that history shows are

"*WHAT WORKS*"

Since human nature is the essential moving force in achieving goals, it is critical to identify some examples of humankind's propensities that we will have to overcome if we desire to change any part of the status quo. I am listing below some of humankind's major challenges that we must deal with in evaluating whether any proposed or desired action is likely to be achievable:

1. Each person is predominantly influenced by what is in "*the best interests of one's self*."
2. Humans are motivated to produce the best quality and the most quantity when they are offered *incentives*. Other methodologies (such as accountability and punishment) have yielded much poorer results.

3. People tend to *"prefer present gratifica-tion"* and *"oppose deferred gratification."*

4. Many people believe that funds received from their government are *"FREE"* and not funds that were forcibly taken by government from others who earned them. Nevertheless, we all continue to mistakenly subscribe to the belief that there are no such things as *"free lunches"* in this world. (See relevant comment below)

5. Most people prefer to avoid working if *they can get someone else to do a desired job*. (See relevant comment below)

Comment on point 4 above - - - A national USA newspaper published the following observation:

"The presumption implicit in the criticism of growing economic inequality *is that society's income is a given* and, if the rich have less, others will have more. Up to a point, that's true. The government already redistributes much income, often for the good. But the redistributionist argument is, at best, a half-truth. *The larger truth is that much of the income of the rich and well-to-do comes from what they have created with*

their talent and capital and which they continue to support. If they stop doing it, then the income and wealth vanish. No one gets it. It can't be redistributed because it doesn't exist. Everyone's poorer" !!!

Comment on point 5 above - - - A humorous depiction of how the issue sometimes works is shown below:

There were four people named Everybody, Somebody, Anybody and Nobody. There was an important job to be done and Everybody was sure Somebody would do it. Anybody could have done it, but Nobody did it. Somebody got angry about that, because it was Everybody's job. Everybody thought Anybody could do it but Nobody realized that Everybody wouldn't do it. *It ended up that Everybody blamed Somebody when Nobody did what Anybody could have done.*

As I have previously said, I am a **REALIST** and, therefore, I think *it is essential that we learn from History "what works"* when making life decisions in a world that is forever changing. Often, while the facts in a current challenge may not be identical to what we have experienced before, we can still use knowledge that we _and others_ have gained from some historic event to help show us how to best deal with a "_new_" current problem. A wise USA President once responded to a woman who was aggrieved about how to deal with something that she had never seen happen before, by telling her "_the only thing that has not happened before is what never happened to you; it surely has happened to someone else._"

Based upon my experience and history, the economic system that does _the greatest good for the greatest number of people_, in any society, is the Capitalistic model adopted by the USA over 240 years ago. What I cited in "political systems" cannot be overstated: an internationally-respected world leader (Winston Churchill) was once asked to compare Capitalism and Socialism and responded - - _Capitalism is the UNEQUAL distribution of WEALTH and Socialism is the EQUAL distribution of POVERTY._ I concur completely with him after seeing what has been happening in the **REAL** world and what I have reasoned out using accepted and proven theories. Accordingly, I am listing below some of the major advantages and shortcomings of each economic system:

CAPITALISM (*How it usually works*)

a. It provides greater personal liberty than any other system tried to date (except for anarchy).

b. It provides multiple opportunities for members to own property and to seek their personally preferred career and goals and thereby promotes invention and innovation.

c. It promotes competition which has always been shown to be a force that continually provides the best lifestyle for the vast majority of each society where it has been used.

d. It has proven to be the system that lifts more people out of poverty than any other.

e. The USA (an infant nation at birth) was one of the first nations to adopt a modern form of Capitalism and it has shown financial and social well-being results for over 240 years that are unmatched by any country that has ever existed. Its history is summarized below:

1. It currently holds more than 30% of the world's wealth from the nothing it had at inception.
2. It now has a population that is more than 50 times what it had when it was formed.
3. It has tripled its land size since its inception.
4. It has built and maintains the most powerful military in the world.
5. It attracts people from all over the world who would love to migrate and be part of the USA.
6. It has survived multiple severe economic downturns and major wars while still maintaining societal peace and has transferred political power _peacefully_ 44 times, even during wars.

If we truly believe that we should learn "_what works_" from history, it seems that the USA record is a very good foundation that we should study and build upon.

SOCIALISM (*How it usually works*)

a. It believes that some concept of equality and fairness in sharing the wealth and income of the society amongst all its members should be the primary focus and goal. Personal liberty should be secondary to that goal. Accordingly, all means of production should be controlled by society and individual ownership of property should not be permitted.

b. It believes that each member has a responsibility to put the economic well-being of the total society as a sole primary goal in life and to subordinate any personal desires to achieve that end.

c. It seeks to minimize the income and wealth gaps between different classes of society. To achieve this goal, it must rely on continuously increasing taxes on the more well-to-do so that it can meet the **_ever-increasing_** wants of the less well-to-do members of their society. Margaret Thatcher was a highly-respected minister of England who believed in the Capitalistic system. When asked why she could realistically hope that she could ever defeat the then-existing Socialistic-style system that was giving ever-increasing subsidies and significant benefits to the needy, she responded - - - *SOONER OR LATER, THE SOCIALISTS RUN OUT OF OTHER PEOPLE'S MONEY.*

d. Since universal equality does not come naturally in life, *some outside force is essential* if any society wants to bring it about. History has shown that such a force can only be achieved by creating an *Authoritarian political form of government* where the **ELITE** make all meaningful decisions that affect the lives of the **MASSES**.

e. In 1917, Russia was the first major country to adopt Communism (a form of Socialism) and was convinced that this system would be in the best interest of all other countries. Accordingly, for many years, Russia asserted political pressures on small neighboring countries and successfully converted them to Communistic systems as well. The consequences of those happenings were as follows:

1. As a result of World War II, Russia conquered and took control of over 10 Eastern European countries (plus ½ of Germany) whose economies they also converted to Communism during the 1930s through the 1960s.

2. During the foregoing period and the 1950s through the 1980s, the USA and its allies were providing substantial financial aid to the remaining European capitalistic countries to assist them in repairing their wars' damages and to help their economies grow.

3. During the 70-plus years after 1917, the economic well-being (*and lifestyle*) of the European countries that practiced Communism suffered greatly while the countries that were Capitalistic prospered greatly. *As a result, practically all*

of the Communistic countries aban-doned Communism and adopted var-ious forms of Capitalism.

If we truly believe that we should learn *"what works"* from history, it seems that *Socialism is not a foundation that we should build upon*. I believe that its failure is due to the fact that Socialism is not compatible with human nature. It is based upon taking the product of one group's labor and redistributing an equalizing amount to another group that didn't produce it. *The result is that both groups are disincentivized. The producers don't get what they worked for and the non-producers get something without working.*

Since we know that any system selected must be implemented by human beings, it is essential that the economic system selected contain *economic principles* that are compatible with human nature and that it provide incentives for the people who we expect will implement and sustain the system. Accordingly, I present below a *PARABLE* that shows how *Socialism* interacted with, and affected the behavior of, people who desired to implement *a socialistic program that THEY THOUGHT THEY WANTED.*

PARABLE:

An economics professor at a local college made a statement that he had never failed a single student before but had recently failed an entire class. That class had insisted that **Socialism worked** as a great equalizer and that no one would be poor and no one would be rich.

The professor then said "OK, we will have an experiment in this class on a **Socialistic plan**." All grades will be averaged and everyone will receive the same grade so no one will fail and no one will receive an "A"... (substituting grades for dollars – something closer to home and more readily understood by all).

After the first test, the grades were averaged and everyone got a "B." The students who studied hard were upset and the students who studied little were happy. As the second test rolled around, the students who studied little had studied even less and the ones who studied hard decided they wanted a free ride too so they studied little.

The second test average was a "D." No one was happy. When the third test rolled around, the average was an "F."

As the tests proceeded, the scores never increased

as bickering, blame and name-calling all resulted in hard feelings, and no one would study for the benefit of anyone else.

To their great surprise, _ALL FAILED_ and the professor told them that _Socialism would also ultimately fail_ because _when the reward is great, the effort to succeed is great, but when government takes most of the reward away, no one will try or want to succeed. Could not be any simpler than that._

The foregoing experiment leads to the following five axioms that are applicable in every interaction:

1. You cannot legislate the poor into prosperity by legislating the wealthy out of prosperity.
2. What one person receives without working for, another person must work for without retaining.
3. The government cannot give to anybody anything that the government does not first take away from somebody else.
4. You cannot multiply wealth by dividing it!
5. _When half of the people get the idea that they do not have to work because the other_

half is going to take care of them, and when the other half gets the idea that it does no good to work because somebody else is going to get what they work for, that is the beginning of the end of any nation.

SUMMATION OF ECONOMIC SYSTEMS

My major concern on this issue is that *proponents of Socialism are promising Utopian results* to people without disclosing that history has always shown that *Equality for all has never been successfully attained* while *tens of millions of people have died unnecessarily because of the use of force that was needed to achieve Socialism.* Even Karl Marx predicted that *an Authoritarian dictatorship was an essential element* in the process of *forcefully* achieving his goals.

In my opinion, the fundamental problem of society in recognizing the lack of validity of Socialism's promises is the failure to look at the simplest of truths when dealing with the realities of economics: namely, that *the only wealth that can be distributed to members of a society is limited to the amount of wealth that has been created by members of that society.* *Society's members must be incentivized to create wealth before it can be distributed!!!*

In other words, the following equation cannot be violated on any sustainable basis

Wealth created = Wealth disbursed

The problem is that "proponents of Socialism"

only look at what they want to distribute and they assume that the existing wealth will always be there and grow even if the producers of that wealth have little incentive to continue to risk the time, money and capital needed to create and maintain the wealth desired to distribute. History has clearly shown that such assumptions have no credibility at all. History has consistently shown that the wealth that was formerly being created diminishes rapidly and therefore:

> _No society can distribute what no longer exists_
> _and, if it tries, that society_
> _becomes another historical failure statistic._

In effect, the people who are undereducated on this issue and the younger populations who are not aware of the disastrous history of societies who have adopted (_and then abandoned_) Socialism are all being seduced by the _illusions_ that are being promulgated by the ideologues of Socialism.

I urge all of you to become "REALISTS" and let the facts generate your values and judgment whenever you have to make decisions on this or any other matter.

Value Systems

Constructive Functioning in
the Real World

In the course of having lived for so many years beyond the norm, I came to recognize how much my understanding of the meaningfulness of life's relationships, happenings and opportunities had changed as I grew older. I now believe that this maturing process is normal and happens to many people as they have more life experiences. To coin a phrase, I now have an "**OLDER MIND**" that is able to see life more fully in the context of *more* time and *more* experience.

My reason for writing this narrative is to analyze and evaluate happenings in the context of more time, so as to help the "**YOUNGER MINDS**" of others to gain the "**OLDER MIND**" perspective several decades sooner in optimizing their lives in the **REAL WORLD**.

To achieve such optimization, we must first acknowledge the reality that each human is primarily focused on how he can get as much as possible in life for his personal benefit (*"perceived self-interest"*) and only secondarily does he think about how other people may be impacted or are incentivized and how these others are themselves able to cope with life. Accordingly, since we live in a competitive society where there are limited resources available, then, whenever any one person gains more than an equal share of any resource, it would appear that there will be a less equal share for each of the rest of us. This is known as a *zero-sum game system*, which is anathema to achieving a peaceful, productive and prosperous society.

Since the foregoing is clearly undesirable as a sound foundation upon which to build a harmonious society, the world has been constantly searching for a constructive alternative methodology (referred to as *"enlightened self-interest"*) wherein people could be incentivized to cooperate in how to share the earth's resources so that *each person would end up as a winner to some degree*. In 1776 Adam Smith produced *The Wealth of Nations*, a book that is considered by many to be the foundation of modern-day Capitalism. This system is credited by many to have liberated millions of people from the ravages of poverty. Smith incorporates the concept of "_enlightened self-interest_" as the **PREEMINENT** basic principle that he propounds in his book.

While Adam Smith's book deals primarily with economics, I strongly believe that "_enlightened self-interest_" (which he defines simply as "_one acting toward all others the way one wants them to act toward one's self_") has positive potential when dealing with almost all human actions and associations. _Since the zero-sum game system is not a sound basis upon which to build a harmonious society, it is essential that we develop cooperative behavioral systems with our fellow humans_ to assure and maximize the viability of life and also learn how to constructively cope with the actions and propensities of humankind that have always shaped, and will always continue to shape, our world.

Almost all happenings and dynamics in the Real World have elements that fall into the following three systems, _each of which will change from time to time._ It is critical that people with competence and wisdom (who are educated and well-informed on the subject) take part in these changes and bring constructive change that is based upon enlightened self-interest to achieve the most desirable results for each system.

Political Systems

Such systems cover interactions between people that are constrained by governmental laws, regulations and political constitutions whose **goals should be to achieve the best balance between liberty and equality that contributes to a more harmonious society.**

This dynamic is covered in considerably more detail elsewhere in this booklet where I show the advantages and shortcomings of the two types of political systems now in use. Hopefully, such additional enlightening will give you a much more informed view when taking part in any future discussions that are intended to make either political system more likely to achieve the desired goals of the society.

Economic Systems

Such systems cover contracts and business dealings among people in the society who believe that the laws being passed would function in such a way as to _help the economic system being used to operate in a fashion that contributes the greatest good for the greatest number of people._

This dynamic is also set forth in more detail elsewhere in this booklet where I show the advantages and shortcomings of the two types of economic systems now in use. Hopefully, such additional enlightening will give you a much more-informed view when taking part in any future discussions that are intended to make either system more likely to achieve the desired goals of the society.

Value Systems (This dynamic is expanded upon in the balance of this section)

Value systems cover all other relationships with others relating to morals, religion, ethics, culture, human nature, societal norms, and all other elements that affect the lifestyle and well-being of people sharing our world. **These facets of life are a constant challenge, and we all must act with "enlightened self-interest" in order to make this world better for every person.**

So...what is required of us to maximize the well-being of as many people as possible in our Real

World? The first thing we have to do is to identify what our problem is. *And sadly...the problem is US!!!* Some of the natural behaviors of humankind, *that are listed below*, are all obstacles that must be altered and/or overcome for us to be able to achieve our goals of a better world for everyone.

   a. People are *firstly and continuously* **motivated by "perceived" personal self-interest.**

   b. People are **not inclined to do anything that they have not been incentivized to do.**

   c. People are lazy and **try to have others do things for them.**

   d. People **keep looking for a free lunch.**

   e. People **rarely use "enlightened self-interest."**

   f. People **can be corruptible.**

   g. People are prone **to acting and speaking first and thinking later to justify their thoughts and actions.**

Our instinctive self-interest is accompanied by an equally powerful instinct and need for social interaction with our fellow human beings. Accordingly, we tend to lead our daily lives in ways most likely to gain admiration from others. One way to gain admiration from others is to help them, which in turn improves their own self-image. Our incentive for helping others is therefore not selfless altruism but rather enlightened self-interest, which recognizes (and foresees) that personal gains within collective _win-win_ situations may far exceed the value of personal gains at the expense of others in a _zero-sum game_.

If you look at the real world as it exists, you'll find that enlightened self-interest is not very widely acknowledged or practiced. However, my life has shown me that in the vast majority of any experiences where I have had positive outcomes, they always included some elements of enlightened self-interest. Leading upstanding lives and consciously adding value to all of our activities—whether at home, at work, or out in the world—can bring us successes far greater than those we achieve by acting purely out of our perceived personal self-interest.

Attitude

Enlightened self-interest starts in our thoughts

and our approach to the world. Given that every person is unique and deserving of respect, it follows that personal responsibility and ethics should drive all our interactions. A positive mental attitude (PMA) keeps our eyes open to our own virtues and resources as well as to the value of others. When we become people worthy of admiration and behave in ways others would do well to emulate, we add value to each situation and every person we encounter as well as our own future life.

Some days it is easier to add value than others. But every burden is a potential blessing in disguise, and every interaction is a chance to add value. In almost a century's worth of living, I've found that those who have the best of everything are those who make the best of what they have. In my opinion, we must recognize that our only choice in life is how we make the best of what is available to us. Wallowing in self-pity or despair for what we lack helps no one, least of all ourselves. As Churchill summarized, "*Life can either be accepted or changed. If it is not accepted, it must be changed. If it cannot be changed, then it must be accepted.*" In other words, only when we reframe our thinking to emphasize how fortunate we truly are with what _we do have_ can we improve the world for ourselves and others.

Family

When awakened in the middle of the night by a crying newborn with a smelly diaper, a new mother or father might wonder how parenthood advances any kind of self-interest, enlightened or otherwise. Why should parents lose precious sleep to preserve, nourish, and comfort another life? While parents might sacrifice expensive vacations, time with friends, and furniture without food stains, their investment of time and resources pays off in the long run—not least in the joy that comes from raising moral children who enhance all of the family's values and seek a better world for everyone. Just as babies imbibe milk, so too do they absorb their parents' investment of enlightened self-interest, the deferred return of which is invaluable. In a more perfect world, every aging parent who once cared for a vulnerable child could trust that the child, once grown, would return the favor in more than full measure.

As the Jewish proverb goes, "As one is at seven, so they'll be until 70." We cannot overstate the family's role in the development of a child's character. Parents acting with enlightened self-interest accept their responsibility to prepare their children for the adult world by educating them on solid moral foundations. While the specific lessons may change from when a child is seven to when they're 17, or even 70, parents never stop teaching.

The deepest lessons are not what children hear but what they observe. Children are expert imitators and emulators of their parents; the most effective way to teach them enlightened self-interest, or anything for that matter, is for parents to practice what they preach. In my life, I learned to do what's right by watching my own parents. Although they were normal human beings with their own foibles, I never saw them act inappropriately or immorally. The example they set showed me how to be fair and just in my thoughts and actions. It's this foundation for a life of enlightened self-interest that I strive to pass on to my own children and posterity.

Income Generation (Business and Compensation)

Like life itself, the income required to exist in this world must be planned for and managed. The same values, principles, and propensities that apply in life also pertain to generating the required financial resources needed to survive. In addition, we must take cognizance of the real world where wants and demands of people exceed the resources available and where personal self-interest, competition and the countervailing needs for reciprocal social interaction are some of the dynamics that prevail and must be constructively dealt with. Economics makes up the lifeblood of the world, business is the lifeblood of economics, and accounting (the profession I practiced for much of my career) involves the inner circuitry of what business is—functionally, prospectively, and so on. I am grateful to have found a field that is so challenging, rewarding and fulfilling.

It wasn't a question of whether I liked the field of accounting; it just happened to fit into my needs at that time and I could see a significant financial potential. So, I enrolled in Northwestern University to study economics. I later found out, by default, that accounting was the best of all the fields I could have picked. I loved the roles I could play as an accountant and I loved the opportunities that I was afforded therein. I'll tell you what I tell lots of people, when they look at me with a very quizzical look, that accounting is one of the most creative fields that one could select to follow as a career.

When you're dealing and consulting with clients, you have to advise them with respect to business development, new products, mergers and acquisitions, taxes, and multiple other areas. If someone is running a successful business, they always get involved in new directions. In those new directions, there are new ways to negotiate, merge, and harness life's moving forces to achieve the best practical outcome: namely, a better world for every person, or the greatest good for the greatest number of people.

The foregoing, along with what follows, begins to explain why I have described my life as a rhizomatic flourishing with deep roots that grew in more directions than I could have ever predicted. No matter how many new businesses and applications you invest yourself in, there's always a little bit that you learn that is applicable in another situation, which allows us to build upon the foundations of our past experience and knowledge, even as our lives and careers carry us in unexpected directions.

In the real world, nothing is permanent except

change, so that in business and life-planning, the two most important words are *"what if."* From an accounting point of view, I like to have an analysis of all of the moving parts that make up the total picture (financially, potentially, and so on). My initial view of any challenge or opportunity comes from what I call the 30,000-foot perspective. From this global height, you may see the totality of the matter that others may not see, and you may discover unique concepts and viewpoints. But if you stop there, you make a mistake, because depending on the complexity and number of moving forces and details involved in an issue, your view of the total picture may radically change from your initial impression. When I delve into details is where my skepticism comes in. I like to pose *"what if"* questions: **What if** I choose a particular path, **what if** I make a particular decision, **what if** I hire or partner with a particular person or **what if** I overlook the consequences of decisions by others?

A ubiquitous question throughout my life, especially during my adult years, is "how can I minimize liabilities and enhance assets?" This requires a well-reasoned analysis of the real world, open-mindedness, a positive mental attitude (PMA), and creativity. An *older-mind* perspective—based on experience and the observation of long-term consequences of immediate actions—sees opportunities to transform liabilities into assets everywhere. While deferred gratification yields fruit in all areas of life, including business, I have found the gratification of accounting to be more immediately tangible than a field such as physics, where you might develop something valuable but it will be three decades before you are recognized for the achievement. In the business of accounting, by contrast, every year and sometimes multiple times in a year, you get real job satisfaction.

For instance, somebody will come to you with a problem, perhaps a financial dispute with a friend. Maybe they're frustrated that a friend hasn't paid back money lent to him, despite many hand-written reminders and reasonable appeals. In such cases, I do not recommend trying to reason the indebted person out of his disbelief when I say that his debt could be paid if he made changes in the way he was managing and that his future personal self-interest would be best served if it accounts for the interests of others. We cannot usually change another person's values that are based on their perceived self-interest, but we can persuade them toward enlightened self-interest by approaching them with positive rather than negative reasons. In this case, you might tell the friend that you understand he's having financial problems, hence the missed payments. Rather than scold or humiliate him, you might say, "If you're going through a difficult period, I want to help you. Why don't you figure out what you believe you can pay each month just so you'll pay something. You'll feel better and the amounts will go down, and everyone will be happier. It's okay with me if it takes two or three times as long to repay the debt. I want to make life easier for you." Now, to some degree, you're coming there with a positive message, not a negative message. Creative thinking and a positive attitude can be helpful in virtually all situations.

Another example from my own life experience: In 1949, when I was first starting out after graduation, it was a bad time for professionals to find jobs. Even lawyers at that time, in order to get a job and gain some experience, had to become apprentices without pay and not be employees. But I kept my eyes open, and after about six months, one of the public accounting firms was looking for somebody to train. I worked for that firm for about four years, never asked for a raise, got good bonuses and continuous compliments for my performance. Then, they asked me to become a partner (with much more financial reward) and that has been the pattern of my professional and business life ever since. In my whole life, I never asked for anything in terms of additional compensation. Whether I was an employee or principal, I always added as much value as I could and demonstrated a full-commitment to the people with whom I was associated and I was well-rewarded.

As I became a partner and developed a more senior-level status I was given the responsibility of working with other business people who were our clients. In a few years, these clients wanted me to get more and more involved in their business activities. The only way they could get me more involved in their businesses was to make me a co-principal. That's how I got involved in so many other ventures. I was only an employee for the first four years of my career. After that, I was always a principal. And just as I had never asked for a raise, so too, the people who worked for me never asked me for a raise, even though they knew that I could afford it. Whenever I have a fully-committed value-added person in my employ, I pay them more than the market and give them extra bonuses. In other words, my partners, as well as my employees, all reap the rewards of enlightened self-interest.

As Sam Walton, the man behind Walmart, writes in his autobiography *Made in America*, "We've been able to help our associates to a greater degree than most companies because of what you'd have to call enlightened self-interest; we were selfish enough to see in the beginning the value to the company of letting them share the profits." Founders and entrepreneurs such as Mr. Walton give equity to compensate and incentivize employees. In a zero-sum world, this would appear as dilutive because it reduces owners' share of profits in the short term. However, existing owners give up equity with the expectation that the future co-owners will grow the business. Most would rather own a small piece of something large than a large piece of something small (e.g. 10% of 100 million versus 100% of one million).

I subscribe to the reality that every person is consciously or subliminally selling themselves almost every minute of every day in every relationship. They are sell-ing the image of themselves that they wish others to see. Accordingly, it's important to motivate the person with whom you're dealing. One of the best ways you can motivate them is to build up their own self-image. When they find the interaction between the two of you rewarding and thought-provoking, it impels them to let down their guard to allow for more effective commu-nication and interpersonal connection. You may not become bosom-buddies with your co-principals and employees, but if you're lucky you'll establish a feeling of commonality and mutual respect. That's what your goal should be in dealing with others in a world where most people are primarily interested in only themselves.

There is no greater waste of time than a corpo-rate meeting in a boardroom full of egos who are motivated by self-interest and blind to the interests of others. By contrast, what could be more genera-tive than a team of individuals who each contribute their own skills and interests toward the achieve-ment and growth of a joint venture? Successful par-ticipation on such a team does not require sacrific-ing our own interests to advance others, but rather recognizing how our interests align with the team.

Consequently, we defer the instant gratification of our ego to invest in a greater longer-term payoff of the team's victory. By collaborating to obtain shared goals, we achieve exponentially more than is possible with our own limited capabilities.

Many who critique the capitalistic profit motive as selfish greed mistakenly believe that the real world is only a zero-sum game. On the contrary, the pursuit of profit is only selfish if my gains require your losses, which is not true. In my experience, the accumulation of wealth represents enlightened self-interest—first, because it generates capital and resources that can be invested to provide new opportunities for others; and second, because it provides resources to our family charitable foundation for use in aiding others to achieve a better world for everyone. The Bible says that "the love of money is the root of all evil," because we should not love money more than people. However, money itself, as a means toward the end of loving one another and improving each other's lives, can be the root of the greater good. My life has shown that respect for others is more enriching than ruthless competition, and that, in business, an eye for common values and shared goals is a greater asset than near-sighted opportunism.

Generally, success in business requires postponing the instant gratification of our own agenda, not for the sake of blind, selfless deference to others, but as an investment in the future, as demonstrated in the following parable.

PARABLE: What Good is Pro Bono?

Libby needs help. After years of tinkering around in her garage, she finally develops a revolutionary device to track down missing keys. She is sure the invention will fly off the shelves once it is discovered by millions of people, including her husband, who misplaces his keys every day. However, to bring it to market, she needs a patent.

Unfortunately, nothing in her electrical engineering doctoral program has prepared her to decipher the legalese on the federal government's patent website; for that she needs an attorney. With three kids, a mortgage, and one income, she cannot afford exorbitant legal fees, no matter how great the potential payoff. So, she searches for an attorney willing to work on a pro bono basis.

First, she approaches Brian who is a partner at the

largest law firm in town and a college friend of her husband. Brian warmly welcomes her, but as soon as she says the words "pro bono," his countenance cools and he grows distant. He says he's already flooded with a full client load. Libby doesn't get the chance to explain her invention before Brian ushers her out the door.

Libby does not give up that easily. A few days later, she makes an appointment at the newly-opened Jackson Law Offices and explains her predicament to the owner, Ruby Jackson. Like Brian, Ruby is already swamped and handles every case personally since she cannot yet afford to hire other attorneys. Fortunately for Libby, Ruby is no stranger to misplacing her keys—considering how long she spends checking her pockets and rustling through her purses, she figures a device like Libby's could save her as much as 30 minutes a week. Even though it would mean more late nights at the office, she agrees to help Libby patent her device and start selling her product.

Nearly two years pass before Libby's fledgling business can pay Ruby for her legal services. Once Libby starts repaying Ruby, however, she doesn't stop. As her company becomes more profitable, Libby sends more work Ruby's way and refers several other inventors to Ruby's firm. Eventually, she puts the attorney on retainer. By adding value to Libby's circumstances and deferring her own gratification, Ruby gains a valuable client and a lifelong friendship—and she never has to search for her keys again.

Love and Morals

Love is the ultimate form of enlightened self-interest, a ubiquitous force in the real world that influences every interaction with others. Love is the single most important dynamic impacting the quality of every person's life on earth. There are myriad forms and definitions of love, including self-love, unconditional love, romantic love, platonic love, unrequited love, familial love, patriotic love, holy love, and so on. However, for our purposes I will summarize love's infinite variety into the following three categories (*that I present briefly in the section labeled* **"Religion, Morals and Love."**)

1. Love includes a romantic connection between two individuals who commit exclusively to one another and feel that life

is incomplete without each other. I loved my wife Esther in this way, as well as in other ways. On a scale of *"1 to 10,"* her inner beauty was at least an *"11."* She personified and enhanced the loveliness of life itself.

2. Love manifests as a great interest in and affection for many individuals (including kin, but beyond the afore-mentioned exclusive romantic partner) with whom you seek to have platonic and mutually beneficial relationships that will enhance the lives of all. To me, this form of love reflects my wife Esther's advice to *"sincerely care for and about the well-being of other individuals."*

3. Love describes a passionate interest in things and/or activities. For example, I loved the roles I played as an accountant and the opportunities that played out in my career. I also love the house on Waters Edge, every detail of which was designed by Esther and me as a labor of love.

My focus, at this time, relates to the love defined in item 2 above. That is, I am using the powerful dynamic of love (*redefined herein to mean "<u>caring for and about others</u>"*) to create mutually beneficial relationships with as many people as possible. In doing so, I strongly recommend that your actions and conduct emphasize and manifest the following themes:

a. Use *"<u>enlightened self-interest</u>"* whenever possible.

b. Commend others in a way that will motivate them and will enhance their personal self-image.

c. Treat every person as unique and deserving of respect and parity at all times.

d. Identify the personal agendas of others and seek to enhance the same whenever possible.

e. Prioritize personal responsibility and ethics. <u>*Be a role-model to admire.*</u>

f. Seek to <u>*add value*</u> wherever and whenever you have an opportunity to do so.

g. Utilize the "Factors That Matter" that were detailed earlier herein.

Now, let's explore some real-world examples of the preceding list. Rather than describe the form of love that is "caring for and about others" as altruistic—which implies selflessness and sacrifice of the individual for the greater good—I prefer to recognize it as enlightened self-interest, because it aims to create mutually beneficial relationships. Among the greatest benefits of love is the way it inspires us to achieve admiration from one another. Love is the most productive and fulfilling dynamic because it motivates us to improve and eventually transcend ourselves in order to connect and create with others. Our love for others compels us to emulate those we admire, while our instinctual need to be loved inspires us to be the best version of ourselves.

I know of nobody who loves anyone more than they love themselves. As a realist, I try to recognize this reality, such that I seek to motivate others through sincere words and deeds of love that enhance their own-self-image. Such expressions of love represent not empty flattery but rather genuine recognition of qualities in others that are admirable, valuable, and therefore loveable. But my care for and about others does not mean that

I love others more than I love myself. When you say "love your neighbor as you love yourself," you're mouthing unquantifiable words which are nice and noble but not realistic. However, accepting the reality that we are inherently selfish does not preclude us from acting nicely, nobly, and with enlightened self-interest. On the contrary, recognizing the instinctive self-interest of every person is a prerequisite for creating collective economic, political, social, and religious value systems that accommodate and enhance the lives of so many unique individuals.

Accordingly, philosophers have long argued that our innate love of liberty would compel us to encroach upon the lives of others, if we did not foresee the unseen: namely, that our self-preservation, which we love more than anything including liberty, depends on mutually beneficial relationships with others. To cultivate such loving relationships requires us to restrain the immediate gratification of exercising absolute liberty, in favor of longer-term peace, stability, and cooperation, which ultimately serve our self-interest. We love others not in spite of but because of self-love. In other words, we love others because joining with them preserves and optimizes our life, and because the joint efforts of our mutual love yield more good than either of us could generate in isolation.

Love is therefore greater than the sum of its parts. In a world of scarce resources, love is the only factor I know that grows when divided amongst greater numbers of people. There are many ways to show your love which cost nothing but can result in a priceless return when so invested. While religious, economic, and moral value systems must be conveyed in writing through logical argumentation and appeals to reason, we can convey love—a ubiquitous dynamic that should be both the foundation and the goal of all the value systems which it pervades— through direct personal interaction. A kind word that lifts somebody's spirits may earn you a lifelong friend and ally. A commitment to love affords us a positive mental attitude (PMA) that can even transform liabilities into assets. Instead of hating and fearing life's multiple challenges—including climate extremes, predatory species, disease, and competition for limited resources—it is within our power to choose love and therefore to preserve, optimize, and cherish the miraculous gift of life we have received. Love is the ultimate antidote to a zero-sum-game worldview, because caring for and about others promotes win-win scenarios.

When I was in public accounting, for instance, I "inherited" three different widows with whom I had no contact before their husbands, my clients, had passed away. These widows had not been involved in their husbands' businesses and needed somebody knowledgeable and trustworthy to consult. Since I was responsible for all their finances, I was the one who could help. In the course of resolving that situation, opportunities for me to add value extended beyond my accounting advice when the widows turned to me as a kind of proxy-husband. They talked to me as if I were him. They talked to me about everything. I became involved in their lives, consulting with them on everything from parenting to living arrangements and even their new relationships with other men. Such personal advice was outside my job description, and I did not expect monetary compensation. However, accepting this opportunity to add value to the lives of others paid dividends, not only through the continuation of client relationships, but also by spreading seeds of love which grow when divided amongst greater numbers of people.

Love makes us happy to see the happiness of others. I smile to recall how my father-in-law once worried that his daughter "makes friends with everybody and brings everybody into the house." Esther was that way; she was like a magnet. Early in our marriage, even before we had children, we started going on cruises. On the first morning of one of our first cruises, Esther got up, put on her bathing suit, and went to the ship's pool. "Come up soon and join me," she said. When I arrived at the pool about an hour later, she was surrounded by six people who were strangers an hour ago but who now seemed as close to Esther as if they were old friends. There's a comfort in being with people like Esther—how they talk, how they act, how entertaining they are, and so on. You can viscerally feel the value they're adding to your life and to the world.

You have often heard me reiterate these invaluable words of the wise woman who happened to be my wife: *"Love life, love people, be sincere, and never cease striving to make the world better for every person."*

Esther's life had a quality—the "Essence of Es," we call it—which people couldn't help but love, because she made them feel cared for, and in turn inspired them to care for and about others. From prestigious business and community leaders to ushers at the opera house, she treated every person with warmth and respect. As far as she was concerned, everyone was her peer, and she was sincerely interested in their lives and well-being. Esther was energetic, gregarious, and I loved her more than words could ever express. I could never love another the way I loved Esther, but I can continue expressing my love for her by heeding her advice to love life and to love people.

There was a woman who my wife and I counted as a very good friend and who we used to see once every couple of months for about 40 years until Esther passed. She is an outstanding and intelligent woman, and a lifelong learner. She traveled in wide social circles, and after her divorce, she was busy all the time. She called me up once around the end of the year. "Hey Nate," she said, "I haven't seen you in so long. Why don't we have dinner together?" Well, after a few months of being much more actively involved in each other's life I had a new thought, because making a date with her was always a logistical problem. Her multiple commitments to other friends and family made the process frustrating to both of us and I said, "I'm used to having a 24/7 relationship with a woman I care about, so I'm wondering if you would come live with me." At first, she agreed to move in, but after a few weeks of review, she had second thoughts on the matter and, after I heard her thinking, I agreed with her.

Our personal history difference was that _she was single for forty years after ending a marriage_, whereas _I was single after almost 66 years of a happy marriage_. She had established a very fulfilling social life as a single and had commitments for at least eight days per week. She said, "Nate, I've given your suggestion a lot of thought. In order for me to do what I think would please you, and what might be right for you, I'm not sure it's going to be right for me." I asked her why. "Because I'd have to change so many of the relationships I already have and I think that would change me," she admitted. I immediately assured her that "the last thing I want is to change you. You're fine the way you are. You've had a good life. You continue to enjoy that life. Forget what I said.

I'm seeking a lifestyle that I think is right for me but may not be right for you. However, I don't think that it would work for me if we continued to see each other as much as we do now, and I would like to continue seeing you like we did for 40 years before." She was very unhappy about that, but she eventually agreed on one condition: "Nate, I want a promise from you that any woman you find, you'll have dinner with me and her together, and let me give you my opinion on whether I think she is right for you."

My friends introduced me to other women, but I am grateful that love allowed my lady-friend and me to remain on good terms, and to turn liabilities into assets through positive mental attitude and effective communication. Love incentivizes and facilitates effective communication, which in turn is key to expressing and preserving love. When asked about the legacy of advice he wished to leave for future generations a thousand years hence, the philosopher Bertrand Russell said this: "love is wise, hatred is foolish. In this world, which is getting more and more closely interconnected, we have to learn to tolerate each other, we have to learn to put up with the fact that some people say things that we don't like. We can only live together in that way—and if we are to live together and not die together—we must learn a kind of charity and a kind of tolerance, which is absolutely vital to the continuation of human life on this planet." In other words, we must learn to love one another, because caring for and about others is in our own enlightened self-interest.

Whether I wanted it or not, I've been given a second life. While I cherish the memories of what I had, I also strive to make the best of new mutually beneficial relationships with as many people as possible. To squander this second gift of life I have been granted would be to forget Esther's advice to make the world better for every person. Instead, I will continue loving life and people for as long as I live. As I have said elsewhere, one must plant seeds even without knowing which, if any, will bear fruit. In my experience, planting seeds of love is always worthwhile, even if the return on investment is not obvious. Indeed, unlike the enlightened self-interest of the business owner who relinquishes some equity to share with employees even greater profits in the future, the enlightened self-interest of one who truly loves is absolutely pure, insofar as it expects nothing in return. Love thus transcends the boundaries of political, economic, and other value systems.

All of the preceding applications of "*enlightened self-interest*" manifest some form of "LOVE" to all the participants. I firmly believe that **LOVE** is *life's single most productive and fulfilling dynamic; unfortunately however, it is very underutilized*. I already see my readers itching to give me a taste of my own medicine by reminding me that "love" is yet another unquantifiable word whose meaning we have never adequately defined. And yet, just as my sense of obligation to share my older-mind perspective overcomes my skepticism that this booklet will do justice to my experience, so too, my sense of responsibility to convey what I have learned about love overcomes my doubt that this unquantifiable word will inappropriately guide future readers.

I would like to share a personal analysis of how I view the legacy that Esther left for all of us when she said, "*Love life, love people, be sincere, and never cease striving to make the world better for every person.*" While Esther's foregoing injunctions appear as four separate clauses, we must not overlook their interrelation. Striving to improve the world requires a sincere love of people, which in turn requires a sincere love of life. One must love sincerely to improve the world, because in a world of scarce resources only the unlimited resource of love demonstrates what we know to be true: that life should not be a zero-sum game and that together we are infinitely greater than the sum of our separate parts.

With modern communication and social media, the right messages can quickly gain millions of adherents, and history has shown that large societies can be incrementally moved by its members who persevere and take affirmative action toward the realization of a creditable concept. Given this reality, we must conduct ourselves in a manner that is admired and respected by many people who may then want to emulate our role-model. It is too easy, and too dangerous, to spread discord and hatred in a world where we must compete for scarce resources to preserve our own lives. Instead, let us accept the challenge to spread love and thereby preserve and promote value systems based upon enlightened self-interest.

Philosophy, Psychology, and The Real World

Including ways to achieve a
more perfect world for every person

<u>*Life is an amazingly remarkable and boundless gift*
that each person receives when they are born. However,
they also get the challenges that come with it.</u>

The gift of life comes with the harsh reality that the major happenings that will occur in one's life are matters that have the greatest impact but which were never planned or expected. In addition, each person has only a very limited ability to shape the positive or negative effect that these major happenings will have on that person's present and future life. Although one's capacity to plan, anticipate, and act is limited, the power of reacting to life with **POSITIVE MENTAL ATTITUDE** (PMA) is virtually unlimited.

Therefore, it is essential that each person develop a fuller understanding of the workings of the **REAL** world being entered and what one can do to optimize the gift of life that was received. Accordingly, we must address the dynamics of our world and how to best deal with the obstacles which we will surely have to confront. Since the well-being of our society is principally a consequence of the *propensities and actions of humankind*, these forces are an essential element upon which to focus.

Nature of Humankind

Every human being is born with several instincts that will likely be the primary moving forces in sustaining one's physical viability and in shaping relationships with the humans with whom he shares life. Without these instincts, the new-born could not survive initially, and the species of which it is a member would become extinct.

As the new-born grows, it must also cope with those aspects of human nature that will manifest in the real world in later years. Therefore, in the following comments, I will detail some of the major dynamics and attempt to show their impact on each new human being and humankind's world as well. *The listings that follow are not intended to show that humankind is either good or evil or right or wrong, but to give us a realistic picture of what is actually happening so that we can seek out plans that might make it better.*

INSTINCTS OF A NEW-BORN HUMAN *(Self-interests that control a human throughout life)*

1. *A need to nurse (to obtain nourishment for life and to preserve its physical viability)*
   As the newborn grows, its needs expand to include a much broader agenda where survival also means seeking improvement in the quality of its life and the attainment of more opportunities that are of major importance in a competitive world.

2. *A need to cry for help from other humans (in order to do things that it cannot do for itself)*
   In the beginning, the needed help is only physical. However, as the newborn grows, it needs to be helped psychologically, educationally, financially,

and experientially to be able to compete and enhance its future life in the **REAL** world.

3. *A feeling of insecurity and fearing strangers and others who are not like themselves.*

   The instinct of xenophobia (from xeno = stranger, and phobia = fear), which arises from a feeling of vulnerability in a competitive world, can be very traumatic and create a strong sense of personal inadequacy in the newborn. Accordingly, parents must continually counter this issue to improve the new-born's capabilities and self-image to help it avoid the sense of feeling rejected.

   However, the newborn also has a countervailing perpetual instinct of xenophilia (xeno = stranger, and philia = love) that conflicts directly with the foregoing xenophobic instinct. Humans are also born with the drive to be a highly social being with strong and fundamental desires for social belonging and interpersonal exchange with other humans.

Since both the last two instincts are ubiquitous to all humans, the _"Enlightened Self-Interest"_ process (that _I recommended in "Factors that Matter"_) is essential in order to bridge this conflict of instincts. By doing so, the coexistence of these conflicting instincts becomes viable and, therefore, people will still have common interests in seeking constructive joint activities that advance the well-being of all humankind.

INSTINCTS AND PROPENSITIES OF HUMANS
(My observations appear in red)

1. Everyone has a _perceived self-interest_ in evaluating any plan of action that affects the lifestyle of members of its society. _(The average person typically thinks: "Are my benefits as good or better than anyone_

else?")

2. People typically seek to have government take on an inordinate share of the responsibilities and living costs of its society because so many people believe that government funds are _"free."_ History, however, has shown that this format ultimately causes governments to grow beyond the resources available to them and they end up financially insolvent with catastrophic results. _(People are attracted to anything that they perceive to be a "free lunch")_

3. People tend to _"prefer present gratification"_ and _"oppose deferred gratification."_ This bias, to optimize the present, has been often shown to cause society to accrue debts for the future that cannot be met when they become due. _(This then creates a potential for insolvency again)_

4. Many people prefer to avoid working if they can get someone else to do a needed job. _(This is just another way of getting a "free lunch")_

5. Are people's actions principally based

upon what they perceive is in their personal best interests or in the interests of society generally? *(I believe that personal self-interest prevails)*

6. Are people politically swayed more **by promises** of desired results or more by advocates who say they have **a workable plan** to achieve those promises? *(History shows that promises win)*

7. Are the majority of people in democracies more motivated by programs that call for more *"equality"* or for more *"liberty"*? *(History shows that most people prefer equality)*

8. After societies have existed for thousands of years, with many differing systems and programs used to govern their affairs, have we learned much from history as to what works? *(Unfortunately, very little)*

Our challenge is also complicated by the following:

Many social philosophers have concluded that people first speak and act based upon their instincts, and then reason afterwards to rationalize what they have said or done. This process goes under the name of "Tendentious Reasoning," which is defined as biased opinions. Accordingly, many philosophers suggest that it is foolhardy to use reason to change people out of any view that they have never reasoned into. You must appeal not to their reason, but to their instincts if you hope to alter their view.

So...are we going to allow the deleterious consequences of the foregoing _"instincts and propensities"_ of people to continue to shape our world? And how can we create constructive plans to overcome these _"instincts and propensities"_ and thereby maximize the gift of life that each of us have been given?

My thinking is as follows:

I am writing this narrative in the hope that I can somehow manage to transfer my _"older mind"_ perspective to younger minds so that they can avoid what happened to me. I got _"Older too soon and wiser too late."_ Toward this goal, I have assembled a list of _"Factors that matter in achieving a better world for every person"_ so that new minds will incorporate these "Factors" into their approach to life and can, by example and persuasion, get these "Factors" adopted by others with whom they have contact. As I say later herein, change can only happen incrementally, and I believe that it has to come from the bottom up and not from the leaders that have been selected by those lacking these "Factors." It is only when enough leaders recognize that they are going to be accountable to an "_enlightened electorate_" who will take "_affirmative action_" that we will start seeing constructive changes in our society.

Essentially, the "Factors" that I have assembled fall into two categories. One category requires you to become more enlightened and informed so that you can make wise choices on matters that will be presented to you for approval and consent from time to time from your leaders. On subjects including politics and economics I have submitted pages of information to assist you in making your decisions. The other category of "Factors" deals with enhancing your life experience and advancing your productive involvement with others that are sharing life with you (such as "family" and "friends"). On these subjects, I have written many pages setting forth my perspective of what has worked for my wife and me and has also worked well for others that we have known over many, many decades.

After living in the **REAL** world for over 90 years and studying history, I have concluded that absolutely nothing in this world is permanent except death. This includes all living beings and things, all societies, nations, beliefs, the world we live in, the cosmos we see and just about anything that anyone can think of. _Accordingly, if we are not happy with something, then the only choice we have is to try to change it_ and (as happens with everything else in the world) it can only be changed incrementally.

History has shown that a society can effect revolutionary changes when as little as 2% of its adult population has concurred on such changes and that 2% then takes strong affirmative actions to force the **ELITE** to see that it is in the personal self-interest of the **ELITES** to take action to bring the agreed goals into reality. Accordingly, the world can be incrementally changed, from the bottom up, if enough well-educated and informed individuals (and their contacts) concur with desired goals and join in with the use of social media and other modern networking capabilities to become a meaningful percentage of the society.

However, we must remember that this can only happen if there is an electorate who is not apathetic or complacent and who believes in taking affirmative action to hold its elected leaders accountable!!!

Religion, Morality and Love

Pathways available for humans
to optimize their time on earth

Humankind's existence has always been significantly impacted by two *"man-conceived"* concepts (*or systems*) called **Religion** and **Morality**, each of which, in one form or another, has been a part of every society that has existed and has greatly enhanced civilization's well-being. This chapter also includes a discussion of **Love**, which is the foundation of religion and morality, and which, in my opinion, is the single most important dynamic impacting the quality of everyone's life on earth.

I will address **Religion**, **Morality** and **Love** simultaneously because they all promote the development of systems of ethics, values, beliefs and behaviors (*based on history*) that have enhanced life for humans in the crowded, competitive and hostile world that we have inherited. I strongly believe

117

that the recommendations of these systems have constructively guided humankind to provide a better life for very large majorities of people. Each of these systems has been and continues to be significantly influential for billions of people, and I believe that it would be helpful to analyze why so many have felt that these systems **conceived by humankind** (and, in my opinion, not by a deity) have been indispensable to humans.

Again, I include **Love** because my life experience has convinced me over and over, in various situations and relationships, that **Love** is the single most dynamic and efficacious factor in attaining desired ends and achieving a better world for every person.

Religious Systems *(Origin and current relevance)*

I know that many people believe that Religion has a dark side as well, in that, over the centuries, millions of people have died because some heretics insisted that non-believers must be eliminated. This is historically true; however, I am convinced that *but for the equitable morals and rules promulgated by monotheistic religions*, society would not have experienced such astounding growth and improvement in its well-being, and that our losses to heretics would have been vastly greater.

Let me start by stating that I was born a Jew and that life has convinced me that I was fortunate to have been heir to the values, history and culture of Judaism. I intend to remain in this faith for as long as I live. I am also convinced that the majority of other monotheistic religions with ethical and constructive values will likewise continue to advance civilization to greater heights.

At least two out of every three people in the world today identify with, or participate in, *"monotheistic religious beliefs and cultures."* Such adherents believe that the world and the species that inhabit it were created by *"some intelligent and omnipotent eternal entity"* to which they give a special name (i.e. **GOD, ALLAH**, etc.) The truth of this belief is impossible to prove and therefore requires a *"leap of faith"* by those who accept and subscribe to its dictates. Most members who so identify also believe that their faith and beliefs stem from religious texts that originated from each of their respective GODs (i.e. Bible, Koran, Torah, etc.) and must be observed by each member.

At this point, I would like to explain an apparent contradiction in how I think. I have repeatedly stated in my writings herein that I am a **REALIST** and that I come to conclusions based on *"facts"* and *"what works."* So, how is that compatible with having to make a *"leap of faith"* in order to subscribe to any religious system? My answer is that in my numerous interactions with great numbers of individuals and families who had strong religious feelings, I came away with the strong belief that these individuals and families were experiencing happier and more fulfilling lives than most other people that I knew. This reality was based on my experience with members of many religious systems, as well as Judaism. Accordingly, if people's goals are to optimize their lives on earth, then the life results that are achieved by people who had stronger religious feelings are truly *"facts"* and, therefore, *"what works."*

In the main, I would like to acknowledge that I am a fervent advocate of most values and behaviors that are propounded by all monotheistic religions. However, I also believe that if one subscribes to any religious faith, it should not require each person to subordinate his ability to reason with respect to any rule that offends his judgment and sense of truth.

So...how did I conclude that Religion was *not conceived by a deity*, but rather **by and for humankind**? My explanation follows:

I believe that when humanity first began appearing on earth, it consisted of multiple small communities that were distant from each other and had no means of communication or transportation to have any connection or relationship with each other for thousands of years. **Yet**, each community developed some form of religious belief different from those that other communities adopted. If there was only one God, why were the religions all different from each other? This led me to believe that Religion must be "*man-conceived*" due to humankind's needs and did not originate from any of the unique **GODs**.

So...what was that need? I believe that humans were traumatized by the reality of death wherein each person would ultimately become a "*nothing.*" In order to accept the reality of mortality, *humans had to have hope for some form of continuity of existence.* In addition, the existential dangers of the world created circumstances which at times humankind could not overcome. **So...**man needed to hope that some all-powerful external force could provide salvation. Accordingly, Religion provided the concept of an _afterlife_ as well as **the existence of an omnipotent and ever-present entity** that could help believers when there appeared to be "_no other hope_" that would solve their then present "_hopeless_" problem.

A very important advantage of the foregoing religious concept was that it permitted the religious leaders to assert that access to the desired "_afterlife_" and "_hope_" were dependent on the degree to which believers were compliant with the morals and beliefs of the related religious texts that were being used. Since the punishment of bad behavior promotes virtue and benefits for any group, this condition was very effective for the religion involved.

In sum, the morals incorporated in _religious texts served a dual purpose._ Namely, to provide a path that was more likely to enhance man's well-being in the REAL world and also create a closer bond to the related religion. In contrast, _a secular morality system (referred to below) focuses solely on humankind's well-being in this world for the present and the future._ In effect, by observing such morals, we benefit from our forebears who have traveled a similar path and have developed ethics, values and beliefs that will assist us in optimizing our time on earth and teach us which pathways we should avoid that are otherwise *"currently unseen"* by us.

Society's Secular Morality Systems *(Origin and current relevance)*

Many people believe that there is some common origin, connection or interaction of society's morality systems and rules with the morality systems and rules that have been promulgated by various monotheistic religions for its members. I have not been able to find any well-reasoned support for that conclusion.

My belief is that all of the morality writings evolved at different times but dealt with similar subject matters to a great extent. Both systems relied, in large measure, on the history of humankind that preceded each of the writings and were intended to better inform future humans of what likely lay ahead for them. Many of the differences between these systems today stem from the fact that religious morality texts are relatively unalterable, whereas secular morality texts must be continually updated to recognize humankind's changes through the generations. I strongly feel that each of us should learn from history as much as possible and integrate the wisdom of the ages into the foundations that are the essence of our own existence. My sincerest hope is that such morality structures become a _social contract for people_, in their interaction with others, _the same as a constitution is for a government_.

I believe that the morals humans possess are partly innate and partly experiential, and to some extent, that which is innate can be altered by nurture and experience. Gary Marcus, a respected neuroscientist, commented on this issue, as follows:

"Nature bestows upon the newborn a considerably complex brain, but one that is best seen as _prewired_...flexible and subject to change...rather than _hardwired_, fixed and immutable."

He later expands as follows:

"Nature provides a first draft, which experience then revises...'Built-in' does not mean unmalleable; it means _"organized in advance of experience"_...

Jonathan Haidt, a highly-regarded social psychologist, has written in-depth about the impact of morality on humankind's culture and existence and he focuses, in particular, on when morals have been a relevant moving force in human behavior. Research in this field by Haidt and others has identified modules upon which various cultures have constructed moral matrices. So far, his work has identified that the following six **Moral Foundations** will trigger responses from people when any related issue is involved, whether it be positive or negative:

Moral Foundations

1. **Care or Harm** (Evolved in response to the challenge of raising children and sensitizes us to signs of suffering and need)
2. **Fairness or Cheating** (Evolved in response to the challenge of reaping the rewards of cooperation without being exploited)
3. **Loyalty or Betrayal** (Evolved in response to the challenge of forming and maintaining coalitions)
4. **Authority or Subversion** (Evolved in re-

sponse to the challenge of forging relationships that will benefit us within our social hierarchies)

5. **Sanctity or Degradation** (Evolved in response to the challenge of living in a world where threats must be avoided and "what works" must be preserved)

6. **Liberty or Oppression** (Evolved in response to the challenges of egalitarianism, bullies and tyrants)

Mr. Haidt (who has had political speech-writing experience) has also attempted to analyze the impact of the foregoing Moral Foundations on people and our political systems. His studies covered a period of about 40 years (*prior to the year 2000*) during which the Democrats were relatively unsuccessful in winning presidential elections. He then studied the political platforms and speeches of both parties and concluded the following:

> The Democrats primarily emphasized Moral Foundations 1, 2 and 6, while the Republicans emphasized all 6 Moral Foundations.

The foregoing compels one to think of how best to enhance peoples' ability to communicate more effectively. Additionally, since many social philosophers agree that people talk and act first and then try to justify what they said or did later, what does that imply if you want to persuade someone, who is instinctively "hard-wired," against any other view? It would appear that one should not expect to reason any person out of any position which that person never reasoned into. *Ergo...you must first get their attention!* I believe that building upon moral foundations to which other people may be sensitive (e.g. *tolerance and respect for all people*) is the best way to begin to communicate with an otherwise closed mind.

I believe that the most difficult challenge in achieving a better world is communicating with others in the most honest and meaningful way. Accordingly, if we can get the majority of people to adopt society's moral structures as a foundation for their behavior, ethics and beliefs, we will then be on a bright path for the future of humankind... which is my most earnest hope!!!

__LOVE__ *(A powerful ubiquitous impact in the REAL world)*

The gift to humans of being born into our world is one of the most amazing miracles that one can conceive of happening. This gift is full of opportunities and experiences for humans to enjoy an exceptionally fulfilling life *(while they are here)* which is almost unlimited in terms of what we can now envision. This gift also comes with the concomitant reality of serious challenges __*like climate extremes and predatory species*__. Fortunately, humans have found ways of keeping such liabilities from outweighing the benefits of the gift that was received.

However, humans have found another liability that relates to the nature of humankind itself and for which they have not yet found an effective solution. This problem stems from humans having an innate instinct to compete with other humans for power in how to share the benefits and resources that are available in this world. The result of this instinct is that when one person is able to satisfy his perceived self-interest by gaining more than an equal share of any benefits that are available, then other humans will have comparatively less than an equal share of such benefits. This amounts conceptually to a __*zero-*__

sum game, where for one person to be a winner, another person must be a loser. Such inequality engenders much unrest among the population. In previous sections herein we have advocated the adoption of _enlightened self-interest_ (**ESI**) where humans deal with all problems by finding solutions that make everyone a winner to some extent. Our life experience has proven to us that this is a viable process and goal which has resulted in amazing innovation and progress in advancing civilization's well-being. However, _ESI_ is not widely practiced among the population and, therefore, its benefits are not yet sufficient to overcome the problem.

One of the principal goals for writing this narrative is to help our posterity optimize the gift of life that it has received. One step in reaching this goal was for us to develop a listing of "_Factors that matter in achieving a better world for every person_" that was presented earlier herein in the hope that readers would incorporate such "Factors" into their dealings with other humans with whom they share this world. Nothing is more important than effective communication between individuals and across generations, which is why I have attempted to capture, in words, my older-mind perspective.

So...what additional steps can we take to reach our goals?

Religion, Morality and Love have proven to be three of the most effective forces in shaping humankind's conduct in this world, and I believe that each, in its own way, can continue to serve us. Religion and Morality convey their values in writing for all people, while Love can best be presented in the process of dealing with persons directly.

So...let me repeat here what I suggested in a preceding section entitled "Value Systems and Constructive Functioning in the Real World," where I summarized the multiple forms of love as follows:

1. Love is being romantically connected with one person as much as possible, and when you are not, you are thinking about being together because you need that person; without that special one, your life is incomplete.

2. Love is having a great interest and affection for many individuals (including kin, but beyond the afore-mentioned special

one) with whom you seek to have non-romantic relationships that are mutually beneficial and which will enhance the lives of all. To me, this form of love relates to "*Sincerely caring for and about the well-being of other individuals*."

3. Love is having a great interest and feeling for things and/or activities.

Accordingly, the additional steps to be taken relate to the love defined in item 2 above. We should focus on using the powerful dynamic of Love (*redefined in this matter to mean "caring for and about others"*) to create mutually beneficial relationships with as many of the people that we share the world with as possible. In doing so, I strongly recommend that your actions and conduct emphasize and manifest the following themes:

a. Use "Enlightened self-interest" whenever possible.

b. Commend others in a way that will motivate them and will enhance their self-image.

c. Treat the other person as unique and

deserving of respect and parity at all times.

d. Identify the personal agendas of others and seek to enhance the same whenever possible.

e. Recognize the importance of personal responsibility and ethics. _Be a role-model to admire._

f. Utilize the "Factors That Matter" that were detailed earlier herein.

g. Seek to add value wherever and whenever you have an opportunity to do so.

Summation:

Since a primary objective in writing this narrative is to help make this world better for every person, therefore, what we offer must attract enough like-minded others so that we become a sizeable enough group to meaningfully sway the **ELITE** (of our society) to make the necessary changes for which we call. To achieve this, we must conduct ourselves in a manner that is admired and respected by many more people who can be stimulated and desire to emulate our role-model. We must also share and spread

Love, Respect and Constructive Ideas as widely as possible. I know that with modern communicating methodologies, the right messages can gain millions of adherents in relatively short periods. I also know that history has shown that large societies can be incrementally moved by as little as 2% of its members when such a group perseveres, takes affirmative action and has a creditable concept.

In sum, I strongly believe that using the powerful forces of Religion, Morality and Love is essential to achieve the better world we are seeking. What is required is that we get enough people to unite with our goals and take affirmative steps to compel appropriate action from the **ELITES** of the world to modify their respective societal systems toward the goals we seek.

Planning and Gratification

If not NOW...then WHEN...
and HOW to optimize one's life?

It is beyond anything that I can understand that the single cell resulting from sexual intercourse between a man and a woman could produce billions of additional cells where each new cell plays a unique role in the development of a human being. It is likewise beyond my understanding that this single cell produces a complex brain that continuously makes the human viable and functioning all the days of its life. It is almost incredible that there isn't some grand plan beyond our ken that causes and controls this miraculous cellular process. To compound the mystery, there also must be a plan to bring the new-born, <u>who (at birth) is totally unable to meet its own survival needs</u>, to the stage where that human being could survive on its own. I don't ever expect to understand how all the foregoing was possible at all and yet seems likely to continue for the unforeseeable future.

Nevertheless, the picture I have described is reality. However, as a skeptical realist I never say "this is reality once and for all," but rather "this is reality as seen from our current perspective." I have studied the past long enough to know that we never learn from history. I have lived long enough to know that nothing is permanent except change, and that even our best plans can go awry when met with unforeseen challenges or opportunities. Accordingly, we are collectively being challenged to take what I believe is a fantastic **life-gift** and **plan _NOW_** to optimize how we will use this gift **for the well-being of this world**. The courage, liberty, and planning of our predecessors yielded an abundance in our lives that risks making us complacent. We must not succumb to the myopia of foreverism and believe that the liberties and pleasures that presently gratify us will always be available to enjoy. The best present enjoyments are often the harvest of seeds planted long ago—perhaps by ourselves or by our ancestors who foresaw the yet unseen: that we would one day enjoy the deferred gratification of their long-term planning, and that in return, we would providently plan for our future selves and descendants.

So...my thinking is as follows:

While we don't understand the planning that brought us to this point, we do know that, in this world, most desired ends need advance planning and not stumbling in the dark. All humans, starting in youth and continuing throughout their lives, will be required to make daily plans and decisions on various matters of varying importance that will affect the well-being of their present and future lives as well as the lives of others. We can plan to achieve a better world for every person by promoting enlightened self-interest—the recognition that **our own individual well-being is inseparable from the collective well-being**. Planning, like enlightened self-interest, requires what some authors have called "mental time travel." Planning is time travel because we foresee the yet unseen future by seeing what has worked in the past. Behavioral and neuro-psychological data has created a growing consensus that our thoughts about the past are intimately interwoven with our thoughts about the future. Researchers attribute numerous advantages to our capacity to defer present enjoyments for more desirable future rewards.

Most of my life I was cautiously optimistic regarding our individual and collective capacity to plan for a better world. However, in recent years I have observed alarming trends of increasing apathy, complacency, ignorance, and short-sighted self-interest. Many writers have concluded that numerous ethical and economic dilemmas spring from our failure to plan strategically to achieve long-term goals. In other words, our value systems are intertwined and the optimal implementation of any and all systems requires long-term planning. It's understandable that humans tend to prefer the immediate gratification of short-term gains—our culture encourages us to seize the day and live in the moment, and it is easier to see what is immediately before us than to speculate on what is yet unseen. Planning for the future demands hard work and strong education, not just our labor but our understanding of what has worked in the past. The failure to better educate current and future generations about what has worked in the real world—including long-term planning and deferred gratification—spells catastrophe for our best laid plans.

So...given that we understand the importance of

planning, what are the criteria by which we should judge the results of any plan that is decided upon? I believe that the _most important criterion is time_! At what time will the gratifications that we seek best serve everyone's interests? The challenge is often referred to as "_Present Interests (or enjoyments)_" versus "_Deferred Interests (or enjoyments)_." So, in reviewing a person's lifetime, what precisely is "_present_" and what precisely is "_deferred_"? Reality tells me that, from the time of decision-making until death, "_deferred_" means anytime, sometimes or all times after the "_present_." However, this ill-defined summation is too superficial. In my experience, there is not a zero-sum tradeoff between present and deferred gratification. Surprisingly, there can be dividends of immediate gratification in the deferral of present enjoyments for future rewards, although such immediate gratifications may not be what we had planned to enjoy. Notwithstanding our distance from the goal, planning is gratifying in itself, because we enjoy experiencing progress, whether it manifests as the increased power resulting from an exercise regimen or from the knowledge obtained from history. Additionally, the older-mind perspective enjoys instant gratification while tasting the fruits of long-term planning. Those who have lived long enough, and those who have studied the past, see the links between immediate causes and their deferred effects. Once we grasp that our present plans have far-flung consequences—some of which we can foresee, many of which lie beyond our imagination—then we can plan accordingly.

The following issues represent some important life goals where the best timing for achieving gratification differs significantly:

1. **GOAL --- Providing adequate financial capability for retirement.**

    PROCESS --- Make a financial plan at *your earliest appropriate time* and then plan for continuous enhancement of the plan at *all interim times*, as circumstances change until retirement has arrived.

2. **GOAL --- Choosing a career and the ways and means needed to achieve this goal.**

    PROCESS --- Do research, *starting*

in your teens, to educate yourself on what career path you would like to pursue. When you have decided, spend the *next year or two* planning viable ways and means to achieve your goal, and then use the *required number of the next several years* to implement your plan.

3. **GOAL --- Deciding where to live and whether to purchase a home or rent.**

    PROCESS --- When your desire or need arises, *start* to do the required research you'll need to help you decide on time, situs, finances, etc. and then *plan in the following years* for how to achieve your goal.

4. **GOAL --- Planning for your desired family lifestyles for different future time periods.**

    PROCESS --- At your appropriate age and maturity, begin to think of what you would like your relationships, lifestyles, and family structures to be at selected future times, and then use *all* *of your future days* to shape your decisions and actions in ways that you believe will achieve your goals. This plan should be **reviewed regularly** in the future.

While I believe that *time is the most important criterion* in judging the results of our plans, we also must consider other moving forces and criteria, such as how and why we intend to achieve a desired goal. In addition to *when*, *how*, and *why* we plan to achieve a desired goal, we must also plan for the unplanned by asking what yet unseen consequences might result if we fail to achieve the desired goal after deciding to forego an alternative plan. Again, the two most important words in planning are "what if." Even when we fail to foresee the answers, the act itself of asking "what if" empowers us to achieve our goals. Researchers have discovered that if we describe our plans in "if-then" terms that detail when and how to achieve our goals, then we enhance our ability to see and act on opportunities. We should therefore plan always to ask ourselves the following: *If not NOW, then WHEN, and*

Planning and Gratification

HOW to optimize life for ourselves and others?

I have long planned to achieve goals that were within my power to achieve, and often the practice of planning enabled me to achieve what had not previously been within my power. Nevertheless, as a skeptical realist I know that planning has limits both in space and time. For instance, I have planned to secure my family's financial future, but I cannot and would not dictate how my descendants invest the resources I have provided. I plan to incentivize my children's commitment to our family foundation, but I cannot plan to micromanage in my absence. We cannot foresee the results of our yet unhatched plans, much less the unconceived plans of future generations. The best we can plan, which may be enough, is to educate our children to keep planning, despite the temptations of immediate gratification, despite the inevitability of mislaid or stymied plans, and despite the uncertainty of achieving our goals. Just as the farmer plants every season despite knowing that many seeds will never bear fruit, we must always plan to achieve a better world, even while we plan for the worst.

As I have commented upon earlier herein, most

of the _major_ issues that everyone must contend with are those imposed upon them by life happenings that were not initiated or intended by the person affected. When such situations arise, the only option available is to do one's best to manage the matter with a positive attitude to achieve the best results that are presently foreseeable and seem attainable. **So...**even if the person did not seek to have this issue impact him, he still has the ability to shape the outcome by the decisions he makes and doing his best to achieve desirable ends.

So...let's list some major planning elements that are needed for making wiser decisions:

   a. Gain knowledge of all the major moving forces that impact the matter at issue and the steps that you are proposing.
   b. Identify and define the goals that are desired.
   c. Set the timelines of when each defined goal should be achieved.
   d. Seek the best creative, experienced and professional advice that is available when it is needed.

e. Recognize the reality that most humans prefer "immediate gratification" on almost all issues, while studies have shown that "deferred gratification" is the primary pathway that has been preferred by most people who have been successful.

f. Try to foresee how your desired plan might generate unseen and undesirable consequences to yourself and to others that may require additional creative thinking on your part to overcome.

Your decisions should focus on the desired time that best serves the interest of all people affected by your proposed plan. In other words, ask yourself whether the plan should provide for *immediate gratification* or some form of *deferred gratification*.

Advantages of *immediate gratification*:

1. Beginning health-related regimens that benefit your body throughout your life, such as the following: Avoiding smoking, excessive alcohol drinking and obesity.

2. Starting exercise-regimens and developing will power to seek and add new

health-enhancing patterns of life.
3. Learning skills that will enhance your potential for a more fulfilled future life.
4. Identifying and implementing pathways for career development.
5. Making plans for foreseeable near-term happenings.
6. Prioritizing happenings in the order of their importance.

Advantages of _deferred gratification_:
1. Utilizing and benefitting from the knowledge that accrues from more experience.
2. Benefitting from seeing some significant events that were previously part of your "unseen."
3. Enhancing your knowledge by evaluating trends that may portend valuable perspective in providing for the future.

All the foregoing is based upon facts, laws and moving forces that are visible currently, as well as what history has shown us to be effective ways of coping with similar issues in the past. History features countless examples where _"the unseen"_ significantly impacts, for better or for worse, individual plans and collective planning. In Homer's *Odyssey*, for example, Ulysses' ship approaches the Sirens, whose singing is so beautiful that it prevents rational thought and drives sailors to shipwreck. However, foreseeing the danger, Ulysses orders his men to plug their ears with wax and commands them not to change course for any reason. He leaves his own ears unclogged but orders his men to bind him to the mast, so that he can enjoy the immediate gratification of the Sirens' song without sacrificing the deferred gratification of safe passage.

Today, one can plan for the unseen by making a "Ulysses pact" in medical advanced directives or living wills, which requires decisive planning in one state of mind or health that will be binding in the future if and when one experiences an altered state of mind or health. We should constantly practice advanced planning like Ulysses, not just regarding extreme situations of life and death, but also involving the deferred enjoyments that make this miraculous dream world even more worth preserving. Enlightened self-interest helps us foresee possible futures when we might not see the world precisely as we see it now. Perhaps now one can conceive of nothing more urgent than satisfying a primal desire to quash one's competition and humiliate one's enemies. But if one plans for the future with ESI, then one can see what is yet unseen: that when temptations pass, tempers cool, and reason subdues passion, former competitors may become allies, and enemies may even become friends.

The following dynamics (and others) may be unseen today but may be foreseeable to a degree and should be considered in planning:
  a. Potential changes in statutory laws.
  b. Potential changes in a world that has been constantly changing.
  c. Economic and political trends.
  d. Interactions with other countries that could affect life in the USA.
  e. Potential future actions, by opposing parties, in matters at issue upon which you may require decisions to be made currently.

I trust that all of us believe that we can attain the best results when we _think and plan first_ and then act based upon our best judgment. Accordingly, all of my foregoing thoughts outline the "*pathways and processes*" that I firmly believe have the greatest potential to help you achieve *the optimal outcome*. However, please remember the following:

While I am providing "*pathways and processes*" to help each of you to reach your goals, **ALL** actions required **MUST BE YOUR OWN**.

I WISH ALL OF YOU GREAT SUCCESS IN REALIZATION OF YOUR PLANNING AND A WONDERFUL AND FULFILLING LIFE!!!

.

Investing

Some relevant principles and lessons of history

Although I had a negative net worth about 75 years ago, and had absolutely no funds to invest, I nevertheless decided that it was appropriate for me to research the art of investing the capital that I was confident I would accumulate some day. I was naive enough to believe that there were established programs and formulae that were effective and could be replicated. This research turned out to be a big disappointment to me at the time because I found out that there were no such reliable programs and formulae. It now reminds me of what I learned after many more years of experience in the Real World as evidenced by the following enlightening event:

> A scientist was asked by a friend how successful he was in his research for the past year. His response was "**Great.**" When asked to elaborate, he answered that he had discovered two theories that didn't work. He then further explained that when

there are multiple theories to explain the unknowns of the future and the world, it is important to narrow down the alternative possibilities and thereby make future research much more likely to be successful.

My life experience has proven to me that the scientist was correct. **So...**while I would love to give you certainty with respect to more successfully navigating life's challenges, I have discovered that "_there is nothing, except death, that anyone can be certain of_." Accordingly, when it comes to dealing with the future and "the unseen," I can only hope to educate you with elements of what I have learned during my life that may assist you in attaining your goals.

The existing financial world has created hundreds of different investment possibilities and formats. I do not claim expertise in any of them. However, I have had significant success in two areas of investments and would like to share with you the criteria that I have used and what I have learned in the process.

These categories are:

a. Investments in equities that are publicly traded on national exchanges.

b. Specific types of real estate where there may or may not be exit strategies readily available for you to sell your property at a moment of *your own* choosing.

But first, let me start with some basic investment principles that I believe are classic and should apply to all investment decisions that you will make:

a. If you have not previously done so, you should take some basic courses in *"investments"* and *"economics"* that will better educate you on the principles and practices that apply to each of these disciplines and will better inform you with respect to practices and principles that I will add later.

b. Limit the amount you invest in any one situation to what you can afford to lose without destroying your lifestyle in case you are totally wrong.

c. Diversify the asset allocations of your investments to limit a major downside risk if many of your investments have common market exposures.

d. Divide your portfolio to meet differing objectives. A major percentage (e.g. 90%) should be invested conservatively with hopes of a percentage yield of single digits and a smaller percentage (e.g. 10%) should be invested with more risk in hopes of an optimistic percentage yield of double or triple digits.

e. Never say that you must take a profit on any portfolio asset, because it may drop in value if you don't sell it now. Remember that you are always 100% invested even if part of it is in cash. If you sell, you're deciding that your use of cash will be more profitable for the future than staying with your investment in the profitable asset you are thinking of selling. You must remember that either buying and selling any assets are each only half of a financial transaction. The real test is evaluating your situation before and after both transactions have taken place and that you will be able to say that you're in a better position for the future than you were before. Remember that _your real objective must always be to keep improving your portfolio to be able to enhance your present and future life and not how much you made on any particular investment_.

f. Do not try to maximize your results based upon market timing. Public markets are notorious for group-thinking and over-reacting on up or down trends based upon contemporary (and possibly transient) economic events. These happenings occur quite frequently and cause extreme volatility and cause many investors to make emotional (rather than reasoned) decisions. Instead, you should reevaluate your portfolio and assess the current macro-economy and take whatever pathway makes the most sense to you. If you have relationships with knowledgeable investors or consultants, you should also add their input to the data you are evaluating and the decisions that you will make. However, if you conclude that the market has over-reacted in driving values downward, this could be a great opportunity to buy assets with a large margin of safety and potential for great future profit. *I DID IT AND WAS WELL-REWARDED SEVERAL TIMES!*

g. History has found that holding profitable investments for the long-term has usually given much better results.

Now, let's move on to specific investment principles that I found were helpful to me in making investment decisions starting with "MARKETABLE SECURITIES":

a. I read the *Wall Street Journal* daily to be more informed on economic happenings and the macro-economic trends. I also read other economy-related papers to provide me with multiple views on evaluating investment-related matters.

b. I have several professionals who profess

knowledge in the investment field that I use to manage parts of my portfolio. I give each of them a limited percentage of my portfolio to manage using their investment style that differs from the others and I can then judge, from time to time, which philosophy is working best for any particular period.

c. Since I am more impressed with real estate for its potential of better long-term profitability, I keep a relatively smaller part of my portfolio in marketable securities. However, I do maintain what I call *"opportunity cash"* to take advantage of situations where I believe that the market has over-reacted on the downside.

d. While the professionals that I use make all their own investment decisions for the accounts that they manage, I personally make investment decisions for a small percentage of my portfolio (marketable securities) using the following decision-making methodology:

   1. I assess the macro-economic trend

for the next 2 to 5 years and try to decide which industries in our economy have the best potential to prosper for the future in that period of time.

2. Then I call my professionals and have them analyze which companies in those industries are the soundest and offer the best potential for gain and the least exposure to loss.

3. I then decide how much of my "opportunity cash" to invest and how to diversify it among the top companies that were recommended to me. This process is repeated about every two to three years.

We can now go on to specific investment principles that I found were helpful in making investment decisions in the "REAL ESTATE" field.

First, a little background:

My first exposure to the real estate field occurred over 60 years ago when I was working for a CPA firm with clients who were general contractors and were constructing buildings for real estate developers. After working together for several years, these clients decided to become developers themselves and seduced me and some others to join them in this new venture. It meant leaving the promising public accounting field where I had already achieved a good measure of success, however, the potential that I saw in this new field persuaded me to make the change. While it turned out, over time, to have been a wise decision, it was an extremely rocky trip along the way and there were times when it could have been a disaster. Nevertheless, now we are here and all of my descendants should be very happy that I made that 50-year trip. But I think that's enough about yesterday; let's talk about our tomorrows that will benefit from what I have learned during that rocky road trip.

Now for principles:

a. The first thing you should know is that

each type of "real estate" is unique. The nature of the business being conducted on a particular site will have a significant financial impact on its economic results and valuations. I have been involved with myriad types of real estate and, from experience, I have come to a tentative conclusion that I prefer residential real estate and storage real estate properties that service the general public. I cannot say that my current preference will always continue to be true since the world is forever changing. Accordingly, you will have to use your ongoing judgment to update any of my current suggestions as you see fit from time to time.

b. I am convinced that being in real estate development is almost an assured profitable investment if the following factors are part of such an investment:

    1. The site of the land location is considered by knowledgeable experts to be an excellent location for commercial development.

2. The physical structure and/or business that you are building upon that land is also considered ideal for that site by the experts.

3. You reserve sufficient **financial staying power** to overcome current "**unseen adversities**" that you cannot control for an extended period of time.

c. The capital you are investing over and above the mortgage is at least 35% of the total cost of the investment. This helps to provide your staying power.

d. Never make financial guarantees to any mortgagee for anything except matters that relate only to your inappropriate personal behavior or matters that are totally under your sole control.

e. When investing in a real estate fund or venture, you should also seek input from experienced close friends and consultants who can help you assess the advantages and shortcomings of the deal and ownership structure. You should also check out items F1, F2 and F3 set out below.

f. If you are joint venturing with another builder (who may be a legally controlling party), the following realities should prevail:

1. Your co-investor should be making a cash investment for its equity that is meaningfully significant to the economics of such co-investor and the financial size of the deal.

2. Your co-investor should have a past success record in the business field and structure that you are building.

3. Your co-investor has always been totally transparent in past business associations.

4. You can take legal control if operations are below agreed targets in various financial, building or management matters.

5. You maintain rights to inspect all books and records and communications with any parties that the

co-investor has hired.

6. Detailed definitions of all appropriate costs and actions are spelled out in detail in the agreements.

Notes from the author:

History is replete with times when a patriarch was so sure that no one had his level of wisdom that he limited the rights of his heirs to investing only in those investments that he could perceive (before death) would always be best for his posterity. This was almost always a catastrophe. I have no such illusions. I believe that one should always be trying to foresee *"the unseen"* but that such efforts must be the responsibility of people who are then living through a world that is in constant change. My goal is to pass on *"processes"* for your decision-making that have been shown to be effective in the past.

LEARN FROM HISTORY!

Epilogue

This section intends to provide a concise overview for those who have not yet read the full text of *Achieving a Better World For Every Person*, as well as for those who will have already read it long ago and desire recapitulation. The following principles—**liberty and equality, decision-making, enlightened self-interest (ESI), freedom of the press and the unseen**—are ubiquitous, if often implicit, throughout my collected thoughts. If my readers understand only these fundamental realities, then all my writing will have succeeded.

Liberty and Equality

The war cry of the French Revolution—*Liberté, égalité, fraternité*—contains an irresolvable paradox in its first two terms, liberty and equality, which many fail to recognize as opposite poles in life. We know that life should not be a zero-sum game, but concerning liberty and equality we must accept the reality that augmenting one must necessarily diminish the other. **More individual liberty always results in less equality, while more equality always results in less liberty.**

Unlike equality, liberty comes naturally, but the limitation of liberty requires such *external force* as is necessary to achieve equality. As observed in "Political Systems," the relative degrees of individual liberty and equality among citizens are the most important dynamics affecting the ultimate viability of all societies. The utopian ideal of equality sought for in socialist-prone political systems, for instance, requires authoritarian force to reduce the natural liberty of individuals, who by virtue of their liberty, have realized their potential to obtain a greater share of resources than others. We have also seen that citizens in authoritarian-prone political systems must merely obey governmental decisions, whereas democratic citizens must obey but also have the right to participate in sovereign decision-making. The critical decision we must make as citizens of a democracy concerns finding the appropriate balance between liberty and equality.

Epilogue

Decision-Making

As fundamental as they are, political decisions about the tradeoff between the opposing extremes of liberty and equality are just one of myriad decisions we all make—rationally, instinctively, and subconsciously—in the time and space between our first and last breath. Decision-making is central to politics, economics, psychology, medicine, morals, religion, and every other field under the sun. We make decisions every moment and in every interaction of our lives, from breakfast menus to business investments, from how we spend our time to whom we spend it with. To decide is to elect one course of action instead of another. Decisions are critical in a world of limited resources, where to afford some things we must sacrifice or forgo others.

Achieving a Better World for Every Person does not preach what readers should decide; it seeks rather to help you decide for yourselves by sharing what experience has taught me about making decisions in general. Decision-making processes require defining problems, specifying goals, identifying positive and negative values of alternatives, and selecting courses of action. Our decisions will never be perfect, nor ever can they be insofar as they exclude everything we cannot see plus everything we decide against. Still, we strive toward _more perfect_ decision-making processes through our knowledge that life is a balance sheet. _Decisions should be favored where positive values exceed negative values._

If we lose a balanced perspective, then we are liable to become "single-issue voters" in politics and in life. If we do so, we risk voting against our own self-interest by electing leaders exclusively for their position on a given issue (e.g. taxation, abortion, gun control), without accounting for their stance on other matters that may strongly and negatively affect us. I do not challenge the prerogative of informed citizens to elect leaders based on particular issues and principles they value above all others. But I maintain that we should not make decisions regarding any single issue without accounting for an array of alternative actions, variables, and consequences beyond those we immediately see or can readily foresee.

Myopia threatens every decision we make in life because humans tend to fixate on immediate gratification at the expense of deferred gratification. In addition, the longer the interim time between any cause and its potential negative consequence, the less negative value we assign to the original cause (e.g. because the harm of smoking takes years to manifest, many people believe such harm does not exist). In some cases, the best decision is no decision at all. On the one hand, refraining from decision-making constitutes a decision in itself. We are always deciding—even when we are not. On the other hand, my experience recommends that sometimes it is wise to defer important decisions. For example, during the traumatic first year after my wife Esther passed, I suffered a paralyzing crisis of my decision-making capacity. Irrational passions temporarily subdued my reason, but throughout this lapse I remained rational enough to recognize my situation and therefore to avoid making any decisions which I could not base upon reason. Following any trauma like the loss of a loved one, try not to make important decisions. After my wife Esther passed, I remained decidedly undecided until my acceptance of harsh reality restored the sovereignty of my reason, and with it my decision-making power.

Enlightened Self-Interest

We must educate ourselves and our fellow citizens to make reasoned decisions about different political, economic, religious, and moral systems. We must not make decisions based exclusively on our *perceived self-interest*, because such decisions inevitably undermine *our actual best interests*. We must also learn as much from life and history as possible to understand the nature and propensities of humankind. As skeptical realists, we never claim to have the full picture. Nevertheless, we must seek to gather as many pertinent facts as we can to approach through imperfect probability the ideal of certainty. I urge you to become realists and let the facts (not passions) generate your value judgments as you make your way through life's decisions.

It cannot be overstated: Life should not be a zero-sum game where my victories require your defeats. Together we can and must achieve a better world for each other by developing cooperative behavioral systems to manage humankind's actions and propensities. Our instinctive self-interest accompanies an equally powerful need for social interaction with our fellow human beings. Accordingly, we tend to lead our daily lives in ways most likely to gain admiration from others. One way to gain admiration from others is to help them, which in turn improves their own self-image. Our incentive for helping others is therefore not selfless altruism but rather enlightened self-interest, which recognizes that personal gains within collective win-win situations may far exceed the value of personal gains at the expense of others in a zero-sum world. By cooperating, sharing resources, and showing that we care for and about others, we maximize the viability of life for ourselves and our neighbors. *Only decisions based on enlightened self-interest ultimately serve our personal goals, which are inextricable from the greatest good of our fellow human beings.*

Enlightened self-interest starts in our thoughts and our approach to the world. Given that every human person is unique and deserving of respect, it follows that personal responsibility and ethics should drive all our interactions. A positive mental attitude (PMA) keeps our eyes open to our own virtues and resources as well as to the value of others. When we become people worthy of admiration and behave in ways others would do well to emulate, we add value to each situation and every person we encounter. However, if you look at the real world as it exists, you'll find that enlightened self-interest is not very widely acknowledged or practiced. Nevertheless, my life has shown me that most experiences that had positive outcomes always included elements of enlightened self-interest. Leading upstanding lives and consciously adding value to all of our activities—whether at home, at work, or out in the world—can bring us successes far greater than those we achieve by acting purely out of our perceived personal self-interest.

Because children are expert imitators and emulators of their parents, the most effective way to teach them enlightened self-interest is for parents to practice what they preach. In my life, I learned to do what is right by watching my own parents. Although they were normal human beings with their own foibles, I never saw them act inappropriately or immorally. The example they set showed me how to be fair and just in my thoughts and actions. It's this foundation for a life of enlightened self-interest that I strive to pass on to my own children.

As important as enlightened self-interest is at

home, it is equally valuable in our professional life, which challenges us to identify and also work toward the goals of our colleagues, supervisors, clients, and others whenever possible. In some cases, this requires sacrificing the instant gratification of our own agenda. By showing that we seek to benefit all parties, we set an example for those within and outside our workplaces. Like children observing their parents, our partners and colleagues may emulate our behavior, and in turn, through their own enlightened self-interest, also contribute to a better world for all people.

If we distilled enlightened self-interest down to one word, it would be love—life's single most important and fulfilling dynamic. In a world of scarce resources, love and respect are the only factors I know that grow when divided amongst more people. As a wise woman, who happened to be my wife, used to say, "*Love life, love people, be sincere, and never cease striving to make the world better for every person.*" While Esther's foregoing injunctions appear as four separate clauses, we must not overlook their interrelation. Striving to improve the world requires a sincere love of people, which in turn requires a sincere love of life. One must love sincerely to improve the world, because in a world of scarce resources only the unlimited resource of love demonstrates what we know to be true: that life is not a zero-sum game and that together we are infinitely greater than the sum of our limited parts, if only we are wise enough to practice enlightened self-interest.

Freedom of the Press

Our country is becoming ever more complacent, apathetic, and dependent. Concurrently, I see our social media trafficking more in subjective spin and less in objective facts. The loudest, most influential media voices now have personal ideological agendas to advance and have become "*news-MAKERS*" instead of "*news-REPORTERS*," who use unquantifiable words to manufacture pseudo-events and contrive arguments that disintegrate as soon as they are exposed to the light of reason. Our population is now increasingly receptive to spin because we are distracted by headlines instead of facts. Without appropriate education, we become ignorant, complacent, and apathetic. In the absence of moral and civic foundations, we fall victim to the unquantifiable words of talking-heads and demagogues who promote their agendas, which historically have always failed.

Education is our only hope to stem the approaching tide of bondage. Informed decisions by an educated electorate are a cornerstone of democracy safeguarded by a **TRULY FREE PRESS,** which itself is protected by the First Amendment to the United States Constitution. In a letter to Colonel Edward Carrington dated January 16, 1787, Thomas Jefferson conveyed just how fundamental a free press and an educated public are to the democratic experiment, which was then in its vulnerable infancy and which now, 243 years later, is perhaps even more vulnerable. According to Jefferson, "were it left to me to decide whether we should have a government without newspapers, or newspapers without a government, I should not hesitate a moment to prefer the latter; but I should mean that every man should receive those papers and be capable of reading them." It is not enough, however, that an educated public be capable of reading newspapers—we also need newspapers whose fact-based authority and unbiased perspectives we can trust.

Nevertheless, the absolute freedom of the press is, as all things are, liable to corruption and abuse. Even Vladimir Lenin's communist critique of the freedom of the press contains a warning worth heeding: "All over the world, wherever there are capitalists, freedom of the press means freedom to buy up newspapers, to buy writers, to bribe, buy and fake 'public opinion' for the benefit of the bourgeoisie." In the current moment of American history, accusations of lies and "fake news" are being hurled across both sides of the political aisle. The so-called "mainstream media" has delegitimized itself by becoming a mouthpiece of the left, while the president (not entirely without reason) paints the media as "fake news." Some on the right allow and even accept the dangerous insinuation that the press is now the enemy of the people. Right-wing extremists have resuscitated the historically-loaded term "lying press," first used by leftist German intellectuals and journalists critiquing enemy propaganda during World War I and then deployed by the Nazi propagandist Goebbels, who was unfortunately right to observe that "if you repeat a lie long enough, people will take it as truth." It remains to be seen how the media will regain the public's trust, just as it remains to be seen if the American public will educate itself and future generations sufficiently to fulfil our democratic obligation of informed decision-making.

The Unseen

If I had to summarize the aim of *Achieving a Better World For Every Person* in one sentence, it might well be this: *to focus your attention on the history of humankind and the trends that are thereby foreseeable.* Humankind is naturally prone to blindness regarding the unseen, one of life's constants. The unseen looms large over our future despite being hidden from our contemporary perspective. In other words, we tend to view reality through the distorted lens of foreverism. As such, even when our reason and experience tell us otherwise, we subliminally assume that what we see immediately present before us has always been there and always will be. This mistaken assumption obscures our thinking about possible alternatives, deferred consequences, changes, and latent potentialities.

Be encouraged to extend your thinking beyond

what is immediately visible in the present moment. My long experience testifies that such focus on the unseen will pay off. We possess a capacity to foresee what is yet unseen, although this capacity is imperfect and many are disinclined to exercise it. Such clairvoyance requires just a rational account of the balance sheet facts of life. That is, before reacting impulsively to pursue instant gratification, pause to appraise what currently allures you in terms of how it might affect your future, how it might affect your relationships, and how it might help you become a wiser person. Likewise, before acting according to the whims of self-interest, consider what you do not immediately see—namely, how your actions might affect others whose actions in turn will affect you.

I do not advocate hallucinating with irrational faith, nor do I recommend privileging the unseen over empirical observation. I merely propose that our accounts of the real world strive toward balance between the past, present, and future, as well as between personal and collective interests. Not all that glitters is gold. **The allure of instant personal gain must not seduce us to close our eyes to the unseen.** The yet unseen is no less real than the seen.

Indeed, in the lecture entitled "The Reality of the Unseen" from *The Varieties of Religious Experience: A Study in Human Nature*, American psychologist William James writes that all monotheistic religions commonly emphasize the unseen. But whereas the unseen in religious contexts generally concerns the afterlife, my concept of the unseen instead pertains to the present life, specifically our capacity to actualize unseen potentialities through evolved decision-making in a world that is forever changing.

I have no infallible formula for seeing the unseen. I just want you to know that some actions and decisions appear counterintuitive because our tendency toward personal and instant gratification blinds us to the larger and longer-term effects of what we think, say, and do. We cannot predict which foods, fashions, and lifestyles future generations will prefer, but because we know the essential instincts of humankind inherent in every generation, we can reasonably foresee which of our contemporary actions and decisions are most firmly grounded in the historical reality of what has worked, and as a result, which actions and decisions will best serve the future.

We often fail to see, much less appreciate, the

miraculous reality of the present. Instead of covetously visualizing what we lack, we should train our eyes to see the good in things for which we should be grateful. **Those who have the best of everything are those who make the best of what they have from time to time.** My ethical Ten Commandments stated later herein speculate on reasons and causes for my exceptional longevity. Just as influential as my genes, environment, health regime, and lifestyle—not to mention the social, political, and economic systems in which I have lived—is my capacity for gratitude, which allows me to see what to many is invisible.

Maybe I was born with the penchant for gratitude that has helped me maintain a positive mental attitude during most of the past century, notwithstanding global conflict, collective trauma, and personal tragedies. However, long experience and practice have continuously perfected this trait of thankfulness. As I look back from my older-mind perspective on a wonderful life, I can hardly believe how fortunate I have been to arrive where I am. They say hindsight is the best insight into foresight; even so, my vision is not perfect. I have no formula or words of wisdom for how you should view the real world. My sole intent is to help you become more perfect by shifting your gaze and understanding to the omnipresent challenge of seeing the unseen.

Final Comments

It is generally recognized that peoples' lives are mostly affected by happenings and issues that life has thrust upon them and which were not initiated by them. Accordingly, the quantity and quality of life that each person will be able to enjoy will be mostly shaped by how they cope with events for which they never planned but which life will require them to deal with. After living in the real world for over 90 years and having been blessed with one of the most wonderful lives I have observed in a world that I have widely traversed, I believe it is incumbent upon me to tell others who follow me to what I attribute my beautiful life results.

While no person has a guaranteed life span, for reasons unknown, I have been the beneficiary of living longer than any of my known ancestors. For whatever it is worth, I would like to tell you what I believe has contributed to my longevity.

Firstly - - - I have never smoked, I don't drink, I am not overweight and I exercise regularly. _In other words, I nurtured and did not abuse my body._ **Secondly**, from experience, as I grew older and wiser, _I began to live my life more in accordance with the "FACTORS THAT MATTER IN ACHIEVING A BETTER WORLD FOR EVERY PERSON"_ that was listed earlier herein.

Based Upon What I Learned In Life, I Highly Recommend The Following "10 Commandments"

ADD VALUE TO ANY MATTER WITH WHICH YOU ARE EVER INVOLVED

DEAL WITH ISSUES IN ACCORDANCE WITH THEIR RELATIVE IMPORTANCE

EMPHASIZE THE POSITIVE AND MINIMIZE THE NEGATIVE

SPREAD LOVE AND RESPECT TO EVERYONE WITH WHOM YOU ARE INVOLVED

Epilogue

BE CONCERNED WITH THE WELL-BEING OF OTHERS AND HELP THE NEEDY

BE SINCERE AND PRACTICE "ENLIGHTENED SELF-INTEREST" AT ALL TIMES

ALWAYS MAKE THE BEST OF WHAT YOU ACTUALLY HAVE FROM TIME-TO-TIME

MAINTAIN AN OPTIMISTIC AND POSITIVE MENTAL ATTITUDE THROUGHOUT LIFE

LENGTHEN YOUR LIFETIME BY NOURISHING AND NOT ABUSING YOUR BODY

INCORPORATE ALL THE "FACTORS THAT MATTER" INTO YOUR CONDUCT OF LIFE

**I WISH FOR EVERYONE
AS GOOD A LIFE EXPERIENCE
AS I HAVE HAD IN THIS DREAM WORLD**

AN EDUCATED AND INFORMED ELECTORATE IS OUR ONLY HOPE

Without such an electorate, we cannot stem the approaching tide of bondage set out below. In 1770, Alexander Fraser Tyler concluded that democracy is not a permanent form of government. He found that each of the democratic republics went through each of the following stages in the sequence shown:

Bondage to spiritual faith;
Spiritual faith to great courage;
Courage to liberty;
Liberty to abundance;
Abundance to complacency;
Complacency to apathy;
Apathy to dependence;
Dependence back into bondage.

We must heed and react to the reality that ALL democratic republics, without exception, have passed through this cyclical progression.

Our Philosophy

We believe that life-writing is essential to living; that writing life is a privilege, right, and responsibility; that written words captivate the atmosphere of lived experience; that there are as many styles of life-writing as there are lives.

We are zealous preservers of memories and legacies. Preservation is not just the recollection of ancestors and origins, but also pre-serving: a proactive form of service for family, community, and posterity. Our mission is to create narratives that enlighten, entertain, and inspire while preserving stories that are vital to life.

bioGraphbook.com

www.ingramcontent.com/pod-product-compliance
Lightning Source LLC
Chambersburg PA
CBHW022059190326
41520CB00031B/618